MARK ROSEN'S BOOK OF
MINNESOTA
SPORTS
LISTS

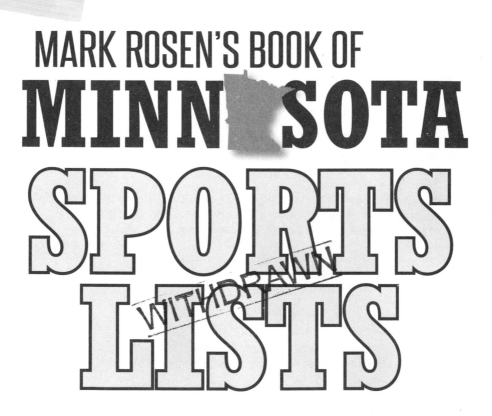

A Compilation of Bests, Worsts, and Head-Scratchers from the Worlds of Baseball, Football, Basketball, Hockey, and More

Mark Rosen and Jim Bruton

First published in 2014 by MVP Books, an imprint of Quarto Publishing Group USA Inc.,
400 First Avenue North, Suite 400, Minneapolis, MN 55401 USA

MVP Books titles are also available at discounts in bulk quantity for industrial or sales-promotional
use. For details write to Special Sales Manager at Quarto Publishing Group USA Inc.,
400 First Avenue North, Suite 400, Minneapolis, MN 55401 USA.

To find out more about our books, visit us online at www.mvpbooks.com.

ISBN-13: 978-0-7603-4580-1

Library of Congress Cataloging-in-Publication Data
Rosen, Mark, 1951-
  Mark Rosen's book of Minnesota sports lists : a compilation of bests, worsts, and head-scratchers
from the worlds of baseball, football, basketball, hockey, and more / Mark Rosen and Jim Bruton.
    pages cm
  Summary: "A compilation of rankings by broadcaster Mark Rosen that list bests, worsts, and more
from decades of Minnesota sports"-- Provided by publisher.
  ISBN 978-0-7603-4580-1 (paperback)
  1. Sports--Minnesota--Miscellanea. I. Rosen, Mark, 1951- II. Title. III. Title: Book of Minnesota
sports lists.
  GV584.M65B78 2014
  796.09776--dc23
                        2014005963

Editor: Josh Leventhal
Design Manager: James Kegley
Layout Designer: Kim Winscher

Back cover photo Sean Skinner

Printed in USA

10 9 8 7 6 5 4 3 2 1

CONTENTS

BASKETBALL

WRESTLING

MORE OF MY FAVORITE THINGS

PREFACE

Everyone has favorites and wonderful memories when it comes to sports, whether amateur or professional. It might be a favorite person, movie, restaurant, city, athlete, or book. Maybe it is a favorite team or a great quarterback, running back, pitcher, catcher, center, or goalie. Favorites and memories are fun to think about, talk about, share, and debate. It's what makes sports refreshing and interesting.

In putting together *Mark Rosen's Book of Minnesota Sports Lists*, I focused on those items that brought about great memories to me personally and those that I believe will resonate well with fans with respect to the greatest, worst, and most memorable moments. The focus was on, but not limited to, the Golden Gophers, Timberwolves, Vikings, Twins, the Wild, and the Lynx. This included great athletes, personalities, and coaches who have brought us exceptional and long-term memories to cherish, remember, and on occasion try to forget.

One of the toughest parts about making many of the lists was limiting them to only ten items; in other cases, coming up with even five was a stretch. And the order of the rankings, well, that's really open to debate, even for me each time I look at the lists again. We all have different ways of remembering things, events, games, and people. And we all have our own preferences and recollections. It's what opens up the debates of the greatest, the worst, and our favorites. It stimulates the memories.

In my four-plus decades in sports broadcasting at WCCO television and my umpteen years on radio at KQRS, WCCO, and KFAN, I have come up with a menagerie of sports lists and favorite memories, and I am grateful to have the opportunity to share them with you.

I hope you enjoy my lists and favorite memories, and see if they match any of yours. In the process, enjoy and have some fun.

Mark Rosen

MY
FAVORITE
THINGS

10 GREATEST MINNESOTA SPORTS MOMENTS

There have been some great sports moments in Minnesota history, from the professional to amateur ranks, from a range of team sports and individual accomplishments. To be sure, there are many more than ten great moments, but I had to narrow it down to these ten greatest.

1. USA Hockey Team Defeats Soviets at 1980 Winter Olympics

I don't think anything will ever beat this. Number one forever in my book! For those college kids to defeat the mighty Soviet team was the impossible dream come true! Then they topped it off by winning the gold medal with a victory over Finland in the final game. It was a great moment for all Americans, but with head coach Herb Brooks a St. Paul native and with 12 of the 20 roster spots held by Minnesota kids, it was an especially special and memorable moment for Minnesota.

2. Twins Win 1987 World Series

We needed a championship, and the 1987 Twins gave it to us. It was a great series and a great championship season. The first championship for a professional Minnesota sports team since the Minneapolis Lakers in 1954.

3. Twins Win 1991 World Series

Then, four years later, the Twins did it again. It was just as exciting and meaningful as the first Twins championship—and special heroics by Kirby Puckett and Jack Morris also make this list. Not only a great Minnesota sports moment, this also ranks as one of the greatest World Series ever played.

(Continued)

4. **Vikings Defeat Dallas in 1973 NFC Championship Game**
It was a big game at the time and a turning point for the Purple
franchise. A Fran Tarkenton–led offense put the favored Cowboys in
their place in Dallas on national television, sending the Vikes back
to the Super Bowl. I was there covering the game, and I will never
forget it.

5. **Tommy Kramer Touchdown Pass to Ahmad Rashad in 1980**
It seems like just yesterday. The Vikings beat the Cleveland Browns
on the last play of the game, a 46-yard touchdown play, to clinch a
playoff spot.

6. **Vikings Defeat Rams in 1969 Playoff Game**
Another big turning point in Vikings history. The Joe Kapp–led
offense and the Carl Eller–led defense defeated a great Rams team
at Met Stadium in a big playoff matchup that eventually led to the
Vikings' first trip to the Super Bowl.

7. **Brett Favre in a Vikings Uniform**
It was a surreal moment when the longtime nemesis from his
Packers days, Brett Favre, came out on the practice field that day at
Winter Park in 2009 wearing a Minnesota Vikings uniform. I still to
this day cannot believe it!

8. Kirby Puckett Hits Game-Winning Home Run in Game 6 of 1991 World Series

Kirby had long been the emotional and on-field leader for the Twins, and in extra innings in Game 6 of the 1991 World Series, he put the team on his back and carried the game like he had so many times before. Kirby's dramatic game-winning blast in the 11th inning came after he had made a leaping, run-saving catch earlier in the game. The tremendous joy and smile on his face as he rounded the bases is now immortalized in a statue outside of Target Field.

9. Jack Morris Shuts Out Braves in Game 7 of 1991 World Series

Jack Morris' masterpiece in the final game of the 1991 series is simply one of the greatest World Series games ever pitched. Getting the start with just three days' rest, Morris rebuffed efforts by manager Tom Kelly to take him out of the game and went the distance in the ten-inning gem, which ended with Gene Larkin's series-winning hit in the bottom of the tenth.

10. Andrew Brunette's Goal Beats Colorado in 2003 Stanley Cup Playoffs

Andrew Brunette gave the Minnesota Wild its first playoff-series victory with a game-winning shot against Patrick Roy and the Colorado Avalanche in the opening round of the 2003 playoffs. In just the franchise's third season, the Wild went on to reach the conference finals.

MY FAVORITE MINNESOTA SPORTS MOMENTS

There are many to choose from, and a lot of them appear on the list of "Greatest Moments" as well, but this list is more personal and includes the moments that affected me the most.

1. **Twins Win 1987 World Series**
Wow! There may never be anything like it again. We had waited so long for something like this to happen. You have to go back as far as the old Minneapolis Lakers in the 1950s to find the last time a professional sports team won a championship in Minnesota.

2. **Twins Win 1991 World Series**
And then they did it again! Kirby's leaping catch and dramatic home run in Game 6. ("We'll see you tomorrow night!") Jack Morris' incredible performance on the mound in Game 7. From worst to first. It's what dreams are made of!

3. **Entering the Metrodome after the Twins Beat the Tigers in the '87 ALCS**
Fans packed into the Metrodome to welcome the Twins home after they defeated Detroit to advance to the 1987 World Series. It was a night that I will never forget. No one, including the entire Minnesota Twins organization, expected the heartfelt support of the fans that was experienced that night. The welcoming the team received was a surreal moment in Twins history.

4. **Vikings' First Super Bowl**
Quarterback Joe Kapp led the Vikings to the NFL championship and the Purple's first trip to the Super Bowl. They took on the Kansas City Chiefs of the AFL in Super Bowl IV on January 11, 1970.

5. NHL Returns to Minnesota
The sadness that came with the North Stars' departure in 1993 was finally lifted when a new NHL franchise was established in the Twin Cities in 2000 with the creation of the Minnesota Wild.

6. Bud Grant's Return
It was devastating when Bud retired after the 1983 season, but it was a great moment in Minnesota sports history when he returned in 1985, if for only one season.

7. Harmon Killebrew's 500th Home Run
Although it did not receive the fanfare that such moments do today, Harmon belting career homer number 500 on August 10, 1971, will always be a memorable moment in Minnesota sports history. It was a special thrill for me personally to be able to cover that game.

8. Target Field Opens
The Twins leaving the Metrodome for the glorious confines of Target Field brought renewed joy to baseball fans throughout Minnesota and beyond.

9. Gophers Football Moves to TCF Bank Stadium
Another exodus from the Metrodome that can be chalked up as one of the finest moments for Minnesota sports.

10. Herschel Walker Trade
What?!? The deal that devastated the Vikings for years to come and essentially turned the Cowboys into a Super Bowl dynasty is a "great" Minnesota sports moment?!? At the time the trade was made, fans and the media could not believe it—it was greeted as a great moment for the Vikes. Of course, it took an ugly turn soon after, yet still remains a pivotal moment in Minnesota sports history.

MY MOST EXCITING MINNESOTA SPORTS STORIES TO COVER

These were the stories that really got my blood churning when I covered them as a sports journalist and broadcaster for WCCO television. I loved to cover these stories, and they were all so exciting at the time.

1. 1980 U.S. Olympic Hockey Team
I never have been as excited to cover a story as when the U.S. Olympic team beat the Soviets in the 1980 Games at Lake Placid. It will always be at the top of my list.

2. Herschel Walker Trade
Okay, the trade turned out to be a bust of monumental proportions, but at the time it was made, it seemed to be a real blockbuster.

3. Brett Favre in a Vikings Uniform
The moment when Brett Favre stepped out of the locker room wearing the purple Vikings uniform for the first time was one of the most surreal moments that I will ever encounter in my sports career.

4. Bud Grant's Return
It was a huge story when Bud retired in 1983, but it came with a lot of sadness. His return in 1985 calmed the waters and brought a lot of joy back to Vikings fans, at least temporarily.

5. Twins' World Series Wins
The 1987 and 1991 World Series victories were as much fun to cover as any sports broadcaster and reporter could ever hope for. They were such great moments in Minnesota sports history.

6. Lou Holtz to Coach Gophers Football

Lou Holtz coming to coach the Minnesota Gophers was a big story. And then after only two years, he left for Notre Dame.

7. Kirby Puckett's Home Run in Game 6 of the 1991 World Series

One of the most dramatic and exciting moments in Minnesota sports history came with Kirby's game-winning home run. Just when you thought there was no way this guy could do more to win a ball game, he came through in extra innings with a gigantic blast to win the sixth game of the 1991 World Series.

8. Tubby Smith to Coach Gophers Basketball

It was a huge story when he was hired in 2007, no question about that—and not quite so big a story when he was fired in 2013.

9. Jack Morris in Game 7 of the 1991 World Series

Jack Morris put the team on his back for the seventh game of the 1991 World Series and pitched one of the greatest games in World Series history—a ten-inning shutout to capture the second crown for the Twins.

10. Fran Tarkenton Traded Back to Vikings

It was a blockbuster trade in 1967 when Fran Tarkenton was traded by the Vikings to the New York Giants, but it was a much bigger deal when General Manager Jim Finks engineered Fran's return to the Purple. Tarkenton led the Vikings to three Super Bowls within the first five years of his return.

10 BIGGEST MINNESOTA SPORTS HEARTBREAKS

It hasn't been all champagne showers and dramatic victories for the Minnesota sports fan. Why do we have to go through this again? You might want to skip this section if you can't bear to revisit these heartbreaking moments.

1. 1975 Playoff Loss to Cowboys—the Pearson Push-Off

I believe the 1975 squad may have been the best Vikings team ever, so when they lost to Dallas in the opening round of the playoffs, it was a tough blow—especially for the *way* they lost. The Cowboys won on a late fourth-quarter 50-yard "Hail Mary" pass from Roger Staubach to Drew Pearson after Pearson appeared to push off on cornerback Nate Wright in order to get open. With Wright lying on the turf, Pearson waltzed into the end zone with the game-winning touchdown. The ending gave me and everyone who saw it an absolutely sick feeling. Seriously, I do not want to talk about it! So I will stop, except to say that Pearson definitely pushed Wright to the ground and should have been flagged for offensive pass interference—and the Vikings should have won!

2. Gary Anderson's Missed Field Goal

Another Vikings heartbreaker! After not missing a single kick all season long—not one missed extra point or field goal—the usually sure-footed Anderson went wide left on a 38-yard field goal attempt that would have locked up the 1998 NFC Championship Game against the Falcons and sent Minnesota to the Super Bowl. Instead, Atlanta got the ball and went on to score a game-tying touchdown to send it into overtime. Making matters worse for Minnesota fans, the Vikings got the ball back just before the end of regulation and coach Dennis Green called for quarterback Randall Cunningham to take a knee rather than take one more shot at the end zone. The sudden-death loss ended Minnesota's 15–1 dream season.

3. Brett Favre Interception in 2009 NFC Championship Game

Once again, the Vikings seemed to be rolling toward a long-awaited return to the Super Bowl during Favre's first season here, and then . . . enough. We have seen it too many times as Vikings fans. Everything seemed to be falling into place, with the mighty Favre leading Minnesota down the field toward the end zone for a potential go-ahead score in the final minutes of the game. Then, after the Vikings were penalized for having too many men on the field (!), Favre made a desperate pass that was picked off by New Orleans' Tracy Porter. And once again, the Vikings lost in overtime.

4. Herschel Walker Trade

Yes, the tenth "greatest" Minnesota sports moment is also one of the biggest heartbreaks. Although the acquisition of Walker from the Cowboys in 1989 seemed like a great move for the Vikings when it happened—bringing in one of the best running backs in the game—in the end, the trade crippled the franchise for years to come. Minnesota gave up 14 players (nine draft choices) to get Walker, who never lived up to the hype. The Vikings paid dearly for many years for one of the worst trades in NFL history.

5. Four Super Bowl Losses

These each could be listed separately perhaps, but that would be too painful to endure. The losses include the 1969 team falling to the Kansas City Chiefs by a score of 23–7 in Super Bowl IV, which may have been the toughest to accept; the 1973 Vikings losing to the Miami Dolphins 24–7 in Super Bowl VIII; the 1974 Vikings' 16–6 loss to the Pittsburgh Steelers in Super Bowl IX; and finally the 1977 team that lost Super Bowl XI to the Oakland Raiders by a score of 32–14. Four Super Bowls and four losses in the span of eight years.

6. AND 7. Korey Stringer and Kirby Puckett Pass Away

If we were talking about life and death instead of sports, this would be number one. Korey Stringer's and Kirby Puckett's deaths were heartbreaking above anything else. Kirby had long been one of

(Continued)

Minnesota's most beloved athletes, and the stroke that took his life in 2006, eight days before his 46th birthday, was a shock to fans and players alike. Korey's death of heatstroke in 2001 on the football field during Vikings training camp at Mankato shook the Vikings organization.

8. Les Steckel's Year

Taking over for the legendary Bud Grant is no simple task, but after 38-year-old Les Steckel led the Vikings to a disappointing 3–13 season in 1984, the new head coach was quickly dismissed. The franchise had become stable under Grant. Even in the years that they were not playoff bound, there was always a feeling of comfort under the leadership of Bud Grant. When he left and the team imploded in misery, it was like we had been cast adrift. There was no Bud to rectify the losses. Under Bud we were used to winning, and this aberration was tough to take. Mike Lynn ended the misery by firing Steckel and bringing Grant back to settle the Vikings' ship. (His comeback lasted only one season.)

9. Gophers Football Loss to Michigan

In the annual "Little Brown Jug" game in 2003, Minnesota had a commanding 28–7 lead heading into the fourth quarter. The Wolverines scored twice in the first two minutes of the final quarter and then, after a Gophers touchdown put the score at 35–21, Michigan went on to score 17 unanswered points. Final: Michigan 38, Minnesota 35. This was one of the most devastating and heartbreaking losses in Gophers history— and worst of all, it was to Michigan!

10. Twins–Red Sox Season-Ending Series in 1967

With two games to go in the season, the Twins held a one-game lead in the standings as they headed to Boston to finish out the year with a two-game series against the second-place Red Sox. Minnesota needed just one win to advance to the World Series. They lost both games. One win! Just one win! Lost them both.

10 WILDEST GAME FINISHES

Some of the wildest endings in Minnesota sports were wonderful and some were dreadful. Some are listed among the best moments and some among the worst.

1. **United States 4, Soviet Union 3**
Even though there was no last-second goal or last-second save, there never will be anything like the closing seconds of this game as far as absolute pandemonium when the U.S. hockey team beat the Russians in the 1980 Olympics. The hometown crowd at Lake Placid and the millions more watching at home simply went wild.

2. **Kramer to Rashad**
Tommy Kramer's pass to Ahmad Rashad to send the Vikings to the playoffs on the last play of the game in 1980 was one for the ages.

3. **Kirby's World Series Home Run**
Kirby's home run in extra innings to send the Twins to a winner-take-all Game 7 in the 1991 World Series was one of the greatest finishes ever. As the legendary Jack Buck called it, "And we'll see you tomorrow night!"

4. **Killebrew's Home Run Beats Yankees**
In the final game before the 1965 All-Star Game, Harmon belted a two-run home run in the last of the ninth inning to beat the Yankees. I will never forget it—one of the great thrills of my life. The Twins would go on to win their first American League pennant that season.

5. **Brett Favre to Greg Lewis**
In his first home game as a member of the Vikings, Brett Favre threw a 32-yard touchdown pass to Greg Lewis on the last play of the game. Fans in the Metrodome went wild!

(Continued)

6. Gene Larkin's World Series–Winning Hit

Bottom of the tenth inning, bases loaded, score tied 0–0, seventh game of the World Series—it doesn't get much more dramatic than that. Pinch hitter Larkin wins the 1991 series for the Twins with a bloop single to the outfield, sending Dan Gladden home with the only run of the game.

7. Arizona Cardinals Defeat Vikings

"No, no, no!!" That's how Vikings radio voice Paul Allen called it as the game-winning pass from Josh McCown to Nate Poole on the last play of the 2003 regular-season finale knocked the Vikings out of the playoffs.

8. Andersen's Field Goal in 1998 NFC Championship Game

Not Gary Anderson—he missed—but Morten Andersen's kick for Atlanta ended the Vikings' magical season in 1998.

9. Andrew Brunette's Game-Winning Goal against the Avalanche

Andrew Brunette's sensational goal for the Wild in Game 7 defeated Colorado in the NHL playoffs.

10. Staubach-to-Pearson Pass Ends Vikings' 1975 Season

This game could be at the top of the list as far as wild finishes, but again it was simply too painful a day in Vikings history to give it any more recognition. The loss came on a near game-ending play: a pass from Dallas Cowboys quarterback Roger Staubach to wide receiver Drew Pearson for a touchdown. Pearson should have been called for offensive pass interference for a flagrant push-off of defensive back Nate Wright. Belligerent fans tossed things onto the field, and a thrown bottle hit one of the officials in the head. Fans came close to rioting, and the memory of the non-penalty will be a bitter pill for the Vikings faithful forever.

10 GREATEST MINNESOTA SPORTS LEGENDS

Sports legends are incredible athletes who have put themselves on the map because of their accomplishments. They are the cream of the crop, the best we have seen. Some of these great athletes also have made my list of the "Most Beloved." They were fortunate enough, good enough, and admired enough to be considered truly beloved athletes and legends.

1. Bud Grant

One of the greatest coaches in professional football history comes from right here and the University of Minnesota. Not only did Bud Grant letter nine times in football, basketball, and baseball as a Gopher, but he was a member of the world champion Minneapolis Lakers in the NBA; was a first-round draft choice of the Philadelphia Eagles in the NFL, for whom he played two seasons; was an all-star with the Winnipeg Blue Bombers in the Canadian Football League; led Winnipeg to four Grey Cup championships as head coach; and coached the Vikings to four Super Bowls and 11 division titles.

2. George Mikan

The great Minneapolis Lakers center revolutionized the game of basketball on the professional level. Many of the rule changes made in the game were the result of Mikan's dominance in the 1950s. Selected to the NBA's list of 50 all-time greatest players, he was named to the All-NBA First Team six times, won five scoring titles, and helped lead the Lakers to five league titles. Bud Grant called him the most competitive person he has ever known. A statue of Mikan stands in the lobby of the Target Center.

3. Kirby Puckett

There may never be another athlete in the state of Minnesota as beloved as was the late Kirby Puckett. His prominence on the field and

(Continued)

off will always be special in the hearts of Minnesota Twins fans. Puck spent his entire 12-year, Hall of Fame career wearing number 34 for the Twins, during which time he earned ten All-Star selections and six Gold Glove Awards. His role leading the Twins to World Series victories in 1987 and 1991 places him even deeper in the hearts of the fans.

4. Harmon Killebrew

Harmon was not only a superstar baseball player but also one of the most genuinely nice people you could ever meet. One of the true highlights of my career was getting to know Harmon and having him on *Rosen Sports Sunday*. Each and every time was a special thrill for me. And anyone who watched Harmon during his 14 years with the Twins, beginning with the team's first year in Minnesota in 1961, had the special thrill of watching one of the greatest home run hitters ever to play the game. A Hall of Famer in every sense of the word.

5. Fran Tarkenton

Fran was the face of the Minnesota Vikings franchise from its inaugural season in 1961 through the great Super Bowl years of the following decade (with a five-year hiatus playing for the New York Giants in between). From his debut as a rookie in the first-ever Vikings game—when he led the team to an upset victory over the "Monsters of the Midway," the Chicago Bears—through his final season in 1978—when, at the age of 38, he led the league in pass attempts, completions, and yards—Fran stood tall among the greatest and most exciting quarterbacks ever to play the game.

6. Lou Nanne

Louie was a star defenseman for the Golden Gophers hockey team, played ten seasons for the Minnesota North Stars, and later became the North Stars' coach, general manager, and president. He was a good player on the ice and a tough defenseman, and as GM and president was known for his exceptional trades. He knows more about more things than any person I know. Lou is frequently on the radio and television and always has insight into virtually any topic discussed. Besides having a great career and still being in the spotlight, he is a great guy!

7. Herb Brooks

Herbie left us all far too soon. His tragic accident left the sports world in shock. Herb was a great hockey coach and personality. His coaching of the United States Olympic hockey team to the gold medal in 1980 and the win over the heavily favored Russians will go down in history as the greatest sports event and upset of all time. His career was magnified by the events at Lake Placid in 1980, but Herb was a great coach of the Gophers and also coached in the NHL with the North Stars and the New York Rangers.

8. Tony Oliva

Tony is just another all-around good person and a wonderful ambassador for the Minnesota Twins. He is well known throughout baseball circles as one of the greatest hitters to ever play the game. If Tony hadn't had the bad knees, he might still be playing!

9. John Mariucci

You have to be pretty widely respected and very good at what you do to have an arena named after you. And John was both of those things. After starring at Eveleth High School, he went on to play both hockey and football at the University of Minnesota, where he was a member of the 1940 national champion football squad. From there he had a stellar pro hockey career in the National Hockey League and with both the St. Paul Saints and the Minneapolis Millers of the United States Hockey League. He coached Gophers hockey for many years and also led the 1956 U.S. Olympic team to a silver medal. An icon to fans and his players, Mariucci was a special person to the sport of hockey and to the Twin Cities.

10. Jim Marshall

A member of the vaunted "Purple People Eaters," Jim was one of the greatest Minnesota Vikings of all time and one of the most durable players in NFL history, starting 282 consecutive games in his career from 1960 to 1979, when he retired at age 42. He has an endearing personality and was perhaps Bud Grant's favorite player, as well as beloved by the fans. It is still hard to believe that Jim Marshall was released by the Cleveland Browns after his rookie season. Did someone actually think Jim couldn't play?

MY 10 FAVORITE MINNESOTA ATHLETES

The list comes from the heart. These are the athletes who have always been my very favorites because of their personalities, their relationship with the fans, and their incredible contributions to sports history. Some are also on the "Greatest Legends" list, well deserved. Some on the list were easy to place, but the toughest part was leaving others off.

1. Kirby Puckett

Kirby, Kirby, Kirby. There will never be another like him! He was a great athlete and a fan favorite. He gave us so many thrills throughout his Hall of Fame career. The fans identified with him like he was just one of us—so happy, so go-lucky—just being Kirby.

2. Harmon Killebrew

The gentle giant was as beloved and revered of an athlete as will ever play here. Whenever Harmon came to the plate, nobody left their seat at the ballpark or in front of the television set; there was always that feeling that you might miss something special—and he usually delivered. His niceness rubbed off on everybody. He had such an incredible respect for the game and for anyone around him. He was special in every way.

3. Bud Grant

Bud is revered among Minnesota sports fans for his great years as coach of the Minnesota Vikings and as one of the greatest college athletes ever at the University of Minnesota. Just the name "Bud" resonates with fans as one of the most popular iconic figures in Minnesota sports history.

4. Bronko Nagurski

The name alone, Bronko Nagurski, makes him one of our most memorable athletes. And he was as good as the name. He was a high school star in International Falls and then a football All-American with the Gophers. Fans identified with him when he played and loved to wish he was still in the lineup. We can be proud to say he is from Minnesota.

5. Tony Oliva

One of our forever favorites of the Minnesota Twins. Tony's interaction with fans as a true ambassador to the game is cherished by all who get the chance to meet and talk with him. He is a legendary fan favorite.

6. George Mikan

During his seven seasons with the Minneapolis Lakers, George was one of the most dominant players ever to play the game of basketball. He is identified by his fans and by those who only have had the opportunity to read about him as something really special. His competitiveness—Bud Grant said he was the most competitive person he has ever known in sports—brings out the favoritism in the fans' hearts.

7. Lou Nanne

Louie is the best! The former player, coach, GM, and president of the North Stars and local media personality is an all-time favorite. He has become one of the area's fan favorites on KFAN and KSTP radio.

(Continued)

8. Jim Marshall

The beloved defensive end of the Vikings and Purple People Eaters fame is one of the most beloved Vikings of all time. More than just a great player, Jim had an endearing personality that the fans loved, and he was as durable as it gets, never missing a game. He certainly is on Bud Grant's favorites list.

9. Adrian Peterson

The great running back will cement himself and his records in NFL history and will always be a fan favorite. Adrian is as exciting a runner as has ever played the game. His personality and character are strong off-the-field attributes.

10. Lindsey Whalen

Lindsey is one of our best athletes ever and a mega-superstar in the Twin Cities. Her personality and dominance on the court while playing for the Minnesota Gophers and the Minnesota Lynx make her a favorite of all time in Minnesota sports history. It was a grand day for the Minnesota sports scene when the hometown hero from Hutchinson was traded back home to the Lynx in 2010. Her presence on the court is something few others have.

10 MOST RESPECTED MINNESOTA ATHLETES

This category is not necessarily the best athletes who register as my favorites but those whom I think are the fan favorites. A tough list to keep in order and stop at only ten.

1. Kirby Puckett

There is only one "Puck." He hit the jackpot when it came to behavior and skills on the field, and he truly connected with the fans and community when off the field.

2. Harmon Killebrew

Harmon was first-class all the way, in every respect of the game and of life. He was a tremendous role model for everyone. He had so much respect for the game that he even taught others how to legibly sign autographs.

3. Bud Grant

Bud remains a legendary, iconic figure in Minnesota sports history. His demeanor, athletic prowess, and coaching credentials earned him a boatload of respect from his players and fans.

4. Adrian Peterson

His personality, his character, and his athletic prowess make him a fan favorite. He truly does get it. He understands the importance of his work on the field and in the community. He is a "give back" person and well respected for it.

5. Joe Mauer

Joe is hometown, homegrown all the way. There is no bigger name in the Twin Cities than Joe Mauer. Joe has become a legendary, iconic figure in the state of Minnesota. "Local boy makes good" sure fits the Joe Mauer image.

(Continued)

6. Lou Nanne

Lou is as popular as ever with his radio presence and his hockey background. He has done it all. Lou is without question one of the nicest people in all of sports. He is well respected by all who know him and have come in contact with him.

7. Bobby Smith

Bobby was such a great star for the North Stars and so beloved by the fans. He was one of the first real hockey heroes with the North Stars and became an extremely popular player in his time here.

8. Bobby Bell

An iconic football figure from the Gophers' glory days of the past, Bobby still maintains his popularity after all these years. He is an ardent Gophers football supporter himself and continues to hold his dynamic personality and icon status.

9. Tom Kelly

TK was as familiar a baseball name as there was when he was managing the Minnesota Twins. He brought about an aura of incredible respect for his love and honoring of the game. Winning two World Series titles certainly helped with his popularity as well.

10. Kent Hrbek

"Herbie" was not only an outstanding player but also well liked by the fans—and still is today! He has symbolized Minnesota Twins baseball for a long time. Playing the game to the best of your ability and enjoying it as well were real trademarks of Kent Hrbek.

MY FAVORITE MINNESOTA SPORTS CHARACTERS AND PERSONALITIES

Great characters and personalities are about more than just being entertaining. My list is of people who were great to interview, funny, and interesting to be around and who made the job easy. They fit into a class by themselves and bring a smile to one's face when just thinking about them.

1. Jerry Burns

If you are making a list of all-time characters and personalities in Minnesota sports and Jerry Burns is not at the top of your list, then you need to reevaluate. "Burnsie" is the best! Besides being one of the greatest offensive minds ever connected to the game of football, Jerry has one of the warmest hearts I have ever known. Everyone loves Jerry Burns! He joined the Vikings as offensive coordinator under Bud Grant in 1968 and stayed in that role for 17 years before becoming the head coach for five seasons. Just mention his name to someone, and I guarantee that you will see an immediate smile on his or her face.

2. Lou Nanne

Lou is one of a kind, a great sports personality. Louie knows more about more things than anyone I have ever met. He held all the positions with the old North Stars: player, coach, general manager, and president. He is on the radio more now than ever before. It seems like everyone wants a piece of him because he is so interesting and entertaining. I really enjoy being around Louie.

3. John Michels

The former offensive line coach for the Vikings is a real history buff and a personality to admire. A one-time All-American at the University of Tennessee, John was an outstanding coach and a deeply loyal individual. His players rave about him. I cannot say enough good things about John. Just a great guy!

(Continued)

4. Kirby Puckett

When they made Kirby, they broke the mold. He was a great friend of mine and had a personality that was off the charts, and he was a pretty decent ballplayer too. He carried the Twins on his shoulders so many times, and he was one of a kind in the locker room and off the field. Kirby had such a booming and joyous personality that I can barely talk about him without getting emotional. When Kirby died, we didn't just lose a great ballplayer, we lost a special human being.

5. Jim Marshall

There will never be another Jim Marshall. It is a shame that Jim is not in the Pro Football Hall of Fame, with the records he set for durability and longevity. He was a leader on the Vikings defense for two decades and a key member of the legendary Purple People Eaters. Such an incredible personality and character. He was like an imaginary figure—larger than life.

6. Keith Millard

The former Minnesota Vikings defensive lineman makes the list because of his play on the field and his off-the-field antics as well. A first-round draft choice of the Vikings in 1985, Keith was a tremendous player and an even more interesting character to cover. I sure enjoyed him when he played here. After he retired as a player, he went into coaching. He was the kind of guy who always had his motor running. He said what he thought and didn't care much about the feedback or consequences.

7. John Randle

John wasn't even selected in the National Football League draft, and now he has his bust in Canton, Ohio, at the Pro Football Hall of Fame. He played for 11 years with the Vikings and was always a good story. He was always talking, much like Kirby Puckett, and never played less than 100 percent. John never let up.

8. Ed McDaniel

Ed McDaniel played for eight years as a linebacker for the Vikings. I really enjoyed Eddie. He had a huge personality and was a pleasure to be around. He always had something interesting to say. If you needed something to write about, Ed would come through. I often had him on *Rosen Sports Sunday,* and he was always a blast. What a fun guy and an excellent linebacker.

9. Mickey Hatcher

Mickey was a total and complete goofball. He was the character of all characters and made every moment around him interesting. As a member of the Twins for six seasons in the 1980s, he brought life to the team on and off the field and was an absolute pleasure to cover.

10. Calvin Griffith

I would be comfortable with ranking Calvin right up there at the top of the list with Jerry Burns, or he could be sixth or seventh—who knows where he belongs? The longtime owner of the Twins who first brought the team to Minnesota from Washington, Calvin was one of the great baseball characters of all time. I loved to talk with him, interview him, and just be around him. He was a dinosaur in baseball but a giant at the same time.

10 BEST MINNESOTA SPORTS NICKNAMES

1. Bombo
Jesus Manuel "Bombo" Rivera was an outfielder for the Minnesota Twins from 1978 to 1980. He had a great nickname and decent playing ability.

2. Wrong Way
During a game against the San Francisco 49ers on October 25, 1964, beloved Vikings defensive lineman Jim Marshall picked up a fumble and proceeded to run the wrong way down the field to the end zone. Thinking he had scored a touchdown, Jim threw the ball out of the end zone, recording a safety for the 49ers. Fortunately, the Vikings won the game 27–22. Although it was one of the most embarrassing incidents in pro football history, it only endeared Jim more to Vikings fans over the years.

3. Bronko
Bronislau "Bronko" Nagurski. What a great nickname for perhaps the greatest Gophers football player ever. He went on to a stellar career in the National Football League as well.

4. Boom Boom
Bill "Boom Boom" Brown, former running back of the Minnesota Vikings—old number 30!

5. Black Jack

"Black Jack" Morris pitched one of the greatest games in World Series history while with the Twins.

6. Killer

Hall of Famer Harmon Killebrew really could kill the ball.

7. Crusher

Reginald Lisowski, better known as "The Crusher," was one of the most famous of all wrestlers.

8. Moose

They called him "Moose" because he was as big as a moose. I'm talking about Hall of Famer Carl Eller of the Minnesota Vikings.

9. Sod Buster

The local wrestler who lost every match he was in: Kenny "Sod Buster" Jay. He got the nickname because he ran a landscaping business on the side.

10. Horseshoe Harry

Sportswriter Patrick Reusse came up with this nickname for Harry Peter "Bud" Grant, the legendary Vikings coach.

10 TOUGHEST MINNESOTA SPORTS NAMES TO SPELL

When you are in the reporting business, it is an obviously good idea to know how to pronounce and spell names correctly. Here are some particularly tough ones that you need to look up before putting into print.

1. A. J. Pierzynski

2. Christian Laettner

3. Doug Mientkiewicz

4. Brent Novoselsky

5. Devin Aromashodu

6. Mikko Koivu

7. Zenon Konopka

8. Brian Duensing

9. Darin Mastroianni

10. Bud Grant—just kidding!

MY FAVORITE NAMES TO SAY ON THE AIR

There was just something special about each of these names and each of these people. I really liked talking about them on the air and saying their names.

1. Kirby Puckett
Just something about that name.

2. Ahmad Rashad
What a name and what a great player and person. It flows like Ahmad ran with the football.

3. Dino Ciccarelli
The name flows off the tongue. I loved to talk about him on the air.

4. Tino Lettieri
The former goalie for the Minnesota Kicks and Strikers had a fun name to say and was fun to talk about.

5. Seimone Augustus
Say the name a few times. It just flows so nicely. A great name to say on the air.

10 GREATEST MINNESOTA PRO MANAGERS AND COACHES

1. Bud Grant

Bud put the Minnesota Vikings on the map, no doubt about it. He had a tremendous will to win, and he did it often. Bud has always stood for what is right about the sport and had a fierce loyalty to his players. He wanted to win more than anyone I have ever known in sports. Bud led the Vikings to four Super Bowls and won 11 Central Division championships. While coaching the Winnipeg Blue Bombers of the Canadian Football League, he went to six Grey Cups, winning four of them. Bud was the first person to be elected to both the Pro Football Hall of Fame and the Canadian Football Hall of Fame.

2. Tom Kelly

Winning World Series championships with the Twins in 1987 and 1991 puts Tom on the list for sure, but he had more than just winning on his resume. He had a magnificent appreciation and respect for the game of baseball and worked hard at putting his players in the best position to be successful. TK was one of the best and most respected people ever associated with the Minnesota Twins. He remains active in the organization working with young players and as a scout.

3. Dennis Green

Denny won a lot of games as coach of the Minnesota Vikings, finishing with a record of 97 wins and 62 losses. Unfortunately, he is remembered most for the devastating 1998 playoff loss to Atlanta when he had Randall Cunningham take the infamous "knee" at the end of regulation, and because he was not a favorite interview for the media. Having said that, he was an outstanding football coach here for many years.

4. Jerry Burns

Jerry was a fan favorite but also a great offensive coordinator for the Vikings for many years before taking over as head coach in 1986. He is credited by many as the inventor of the West Coast offense, made most famous by Bill Walsh's San Francisco 49ers dynasty.

5. Ron Gardenhire

"Gardy" has won a lot of games in his tenure with the Twins—more than 1,000 by the time this book is on the bookshelves, more than any other manager in franchise history—and led the team to five division titles from 2002 to 2010. He is a steady manager who is well respected around the league and by his players.

6. Cheryl Reeve

The Minnesota Lynx have been a sports sensation in Minnesota. While posting the best regular-season records in the WNBA for three years in a row, coach Cheryl Reeve led them to three consecutive WNBA Finals appearances (2011–13) and two WNBA championships. She has done an exceptional job as head coach.

7. John Kundla

From 1948 to 1954, John Kundla led the Minneapolis Lakers to five league championships. That's right: The Lakers basketball team used to be right here in Minneapolis. Just think of it! He coached some all-time greats, such as George Mikan, Jim Pollard, and (briefly) Elgin Baylor, among others. After leaving the Lakers, he became head coach of the Golden Gophers basketball team. His collegiate career is explored in the following list.

(Continued)

8. Glen Sonmor

Glen was not only an outstanding hockey coach but also one of the great characters of the game, with a passion second to none. After coaching the Gophers and then a few World Hockey Association (WHA) teams, he became the head coach of the Minnesota North Stars in 1978. He really knew how to bring the best out of his players, and he took the North Stars to the Stanley Cup Finals in the 1980–81 NHL season.

9. Flip Saunders

The Timberwolves have not ingratiated themselves with the fans over the last few years, but during Flip's years as coach, the team did become a consistent winner. The franchise had its first winning season in Flip's second year on the job (1997–98) and then in the next seven years as well. He took Minnesota to the NBA playoffs in eight straight seasons, including a trip to the Western Conference Finals in 2004. Most often, however, they failed to get over the first-round hump, which unfortunately has become Flip's most memorable legacy as coach.

10. Jacques Lemaire

When the NHL added an expansion team in Minnesota in 2000, Jacques was the right guy to take the job as coach of this new Minnesota franchise. He brought consistency and leadership to the Wild and had success doing it, leading them to the conference finals in just the team's third season. It didn't hurt that Jacques was one of the greatest hockey players of all time, playing with the great Montreal Canadiens teams of the late 1960s and early 1970s.

5 GREAT ASSISTANT COACHES IN MINNESOTA PROFESSIONAL SPORTS

We have had an abundance of great coaches and managers with our professional sports teams in Minnesota. Here are those whom I believe were the top five best assistant coaches in the professional ranks over the years.

1. Jerry Burns

Jerry was an assistant coach for the Minnesota Vikings for the 18 years that Bud Grant was head coach of the Minnesota Vikings. He was always recognized as one of the great offensive minds in the game, and he served as the Vikings' head coach for five seasons after Grant's second retirement.

2. Brian Billick

Brian was the tight ends coach and then offensive coordinator under Dennis Green on a Vikings team that reached the playoffs in seven out of eight seasons. He later went on to a successful career with the Baltimore Ravens as head coach, winning the Super Bowl in 2000.

3. Pete Carroll

Carroll was the Vikings' defensive backs coach under Jerry Burns and Bud Grant from 1985 to 1989, when Minnesota had some tough defenses. He later became the head coach of the Jets, Patriots, and University of Southern California, and he's now the head coach of the Seattle Seahawks.

(Continued)

4. Tony Dungy

In Dungy's first year in 1992 under Dennis Green, he was the defensive coordinator and the Vikings defense was one of the top rated in the league. Dungy had a reputation for providing a calm demeanor on the field and with the players, which served him well later on when he became a successful NFL head coach in Tampa and in Indianapolis.

5. Wayne Terwilliger

Wayne was the Twins' first base coach under managers Ray Miller and Tom Kelly for nine seasons. He was a well-respected assistant by the players and fans and continued a long career in baseball after leaving the Twins, coaching at the minor-league level into his 80s.

10 GREATEST UNIVERSITY OF MINNESOTA COACHES

The University of Minnesota has been blessed with some great teams and athletes. We also have had more than our share of outstanding coaches. Championships are important—no doubt about that—but being a great leader is also an essential quality when you are leading a group of young people. This list of top ten Gophers coaches includes outstanding coaches and leaders.

1. Herb Brooks

Herbie gets top billing not only for his work coaching some great hockey teams at the U of M, but also for leading a bunch of raw, young college kids to the 1980 Olympic gold medal, including the remarkable upset of the mighty Soviet squad to get to the gold-medal game. The St. Paul native also coached in the pro ranks, with the NHL's Minnesota North Stars and New York Rangers, before returning to college coaching at St. Cloud State. Herb knew the game of hockey, loved it, and brought his innovative ideas to the forefront of the sport. He knew how to win and get the most out of his players. Herb is in both the U.S. Hockey Hall of Fame in Eveleth and the International Hockey Hall of Fame in Kingston, Ontario.

2. John Mariucci

John was the rock behind Gophers hockey for many years and was revered by his players. He was an iconic figure at the university, as demonstrated by the naming of Mariucci Arena on campus. After starring as a player for the Gophers (in both hockey and football) and then enjoying a successful pro career, Mariucci returned to the U in 1952 to coach the Gophers. He remained there until 1966, taking off the 1955–56 season to coach the U.S. Olympic hockey team, which won a silver medal. He finished his career in hockey as

(Continued)

the assistant to the general manager of the Minnesota North Stars, working for his former player, Lou Nanne. John had been a real tough guy as a player and was a tough coach, but he was always highly thought of by his players and teammates.

3. John Kundla

Kundla played basketball for the Golden Gophers in the late 1930s, and after a successful 11-year run as coach of the Minneapolis Lakers in the NBA, he returned to his alma mater to coach in 1959. He led the Gophers to a 110–105 overall record in nine seasons. John, a good guy as well as a good coach, also coached at Minneapolis' DeLaSalle High School and the University of St. Thomas prior to his stint with the Lakers.

4. Dick Siebert

"The Chief" put Minnesota Gophers baseball on the map. After all, how many coaches have a baseball field named after them? His knowledge of the game, as well as those "special sunglasses" that he wore, became legendary in Gophers lore. He will go down in the annuals of college baseball as one of the best ever. He was the Gophers' baseball coach for 31 seasons (1948–78), and his 754 career wins and three College World Series championships (1956, 1960, 1964) cemented his legacy.

5. John Anderson

Sticking with Gophers baseball, John Anderson took over a couple of years after "The Chief" and continued the winning tradition. Always getting the most out of our own Minnesota kids, the Hibbing native has led the Golden Gophers baseball team to five Big Ten regular-season championships and nine conference tournament titles (as of 2013), and he is a five-time Big Ten Coach of the Year. John became the Gophers' head coach in 1982, and with more than 1,000 wins under his belt, he passed his mentor Dick Siebert for the university's all-time record for victories.

6. Murray Warmath

The "Autumn Warrior," coach Warmath was head coach of the Golden Gophers for almost two decades and guided them to a national championship in 1960 and two consecutive Rose Bowls. He coached several of Minnesota's all-time greatest football players, including Bob McNamara, Bobby Bell, Carl Eller, Sandy Stephens, Bob Stein, and others. In 1967, he led the U to its last (to date) Big Ten championship. Warmath was also known nationally for being one of the first big-time collegiate football coaches to recruit black athletes.

7. Jay Robinson

How could you have a list of greatest Minnesota coaches without Jay Robinson? As the University of Minnesota's wrestling coach since 1986, Jay has been a consistent winner. It's an almost foregone conclusion that every Minnesota kid who wrestles wants to be part of Robinson's team. He has become a true legend in Minnesota sports history and may be the best wrestling coach in the entire nation. He has brought many championships to the wrestling program at Minnesota and has coached 30 Big Ten champion wrestlers.

8. Roy Griak

Roy Griak has been around the University of Minnesota's track and field program for five decades and is another of the most prominent figures in the history of sports at the U. His 50 years with the track squad is unheard of in modern athletics. Roy was head coach for 33 years (1963–96), and since then he has served as an administrative assistant. His teams won two cross country titles and one track title in the Big Ten. Roy lettered in both track and cross country as a collegian at the university in the 1940s.

(Continued)

9. Jean Freeman

Jean was a great women's swimming coach at the University of Minnesota. She really knew how to get the very best out of her swimmers. The university's first full-time women's swim coach, Jean spent 31 years leading the Gophers women swimmers, capturing two Big Ten championships and four Big Ten Coach of the Year awards. She had been a member of the U's swimming and diving teams before becoming the head coach a year after she graduated.

10. Don Lucia

Although Don has received some heat in recent years due to a lack of championships, he did win national titles in 2001–02 and 2002–03 and has claimed four WCHA conference titles. He has been coaching at the collegiate level for more than 25 years, and through his first 14 seasons at the helm at the university, the Gophers men's hockey team has an overall record of 344–182–59—a .638 winning percentage. Don also has won WCHA Coach of the Year honors three times. It doesn't get much better than that. He is an exceptional hockey coach and a great representative of the university.

10 GREATEST MINNESOTA HIGH SCHOOL ATHLETES

Impossible!! There is no way to include only ten on this list, because there were so many great Minnesota high school stars. But I gave it a try. See what you think.

1. Bronko Nagurski

Bronko was perhaps the greatest football player in Minnesota history, and it all started at International Falls. The name alone— Bronko Nagurski—speaks volumes among Minnesota fans. After leaving International Falls, he became an All-American at the U at two positions in the same year, followed by a Hall of Fame career with the Chicago Bears in the NFL.

2. Ron Johnson

The great basketball center from New Prague was one of the best. He scored 60 points in one game in the State High School Tournament. Ron went on to become an All-American for the Gophers in 1960.

3. Henry Boucha

The great from Warroad may have been the best Minnesota high school hockey player ever. He had all the skills and abilities and was an incredible player to watch play on the ice. His high school, college, and pro careers (including one season with the North Stars) were magnificent to watch.

4. Lindsay Whalen

Before helping to take the Golden Gophers to the Final Four and then the Minnesota Lynx to two WNBA titles, Lindsay was a dominating basketball star at Hutchinson High School, where she was a four-time all-conference selection while leading Hutchinson to three straight conference titles. The return of this popular athlete to Minnesota to play for the Lynx in 2010 was a grand day for the Minnesota sports scene.

(Continued)

5. Kevin McHale

A basketball Hall of Famer who was named to the NBA's 50th anniversary team for his excellent career with the Boston Celtics, Kevin was a star at Hibbing High School and was named Minnesota's Mr. Basketball in his senior year. He went on to have a great collegiate career with the Golden Gophers.

6. Paul Giel

Paul was from Winona High School, where he was a great football and baseball player. He chose the baseball route (six seasons in the majors) but probably would have been a super pro football player.

7. Brian Bonin

At White Bear Lake High School, Brian was one of the top high school hockey players in the state's history.

8. Mark Olberding

Mark was a superstar at Melrose and became one of Minnesota's best high school basketball players. He was a big, powerful, dominating player.

9. Joe Mauer

Cretin-Derham Hall High School in St. Paul turned out one of the best all-around athletes in Minnesota sports history. Mauer was a star in baseball, basketball, and football at Cretin and was the only athlete ever selected by *USA Today* as the nation's High School Player of the Year in two sports (football in 2000 as a quarterback and baseball in 2001 as a catcher). He chose baseball for his career and was drafted by the Twins with the number one overall pick before establishing himself as one of greatest catchers in the game.

10. Dave Winfield

St. Paul Central's finest! Dave had a tremendous career in the City Conference and went on to greatness in college at Minnesota and in professional baseball.

TOP 10 "CUPS OF COFFEE" IN MINNESOTA

This list is for athletes who had legendary careers in their sports but only brief, if memorable, stays in Minnesota.

1. Willie Mays

The "Say Hey Kid" has to be at the top of the list. Although he played only 35 games with the minor league Minneapolis Millers before being called up to the big leagues to join the New York Giants, in that time he tore up the American Association with a .477 average and eight homers in just 149 at-bats. The Hall of Famer would go on to have one of the greatest professional baseball careers of all time.

2. Dave Winfield

The St. Paul kid returned home for a brief time to play for the Twins in 1993 and 1994. It was a blast having him here! Dave had a great career with the San Diego Padres and New York Yankees and was already a legendary player when he arrived back in the Twin Cities. Winfield collected his 3,000th career hit while wearing a Twins uniform on September 16, 1993. He was inducted into the Baseball Hall of Fame in Cooperstown after a stellar 22-year major league career.

3. Paul Molitor

Another local boy who came home to Minnesota late in his career, and another favorite of mine. I can still hear the crack of the bat as Molitor ripped his hits at the U of M. Another member of Major League Baseball's 3,000-hit club and a Hall of Famer, Paul played 21 years in the big leagues, the last three with the Twins. As a high schooler, he starred at St. Paul's Cretin-Derham Hall.

(Continued)

4. Brett Favre

The legendary Packers quarterback enraged Green Bay fans when he donned the purple and gold in 2009 and led the Vikings to a division crown and just shy of a Super Bowl trip. The future Hall of Famer played one more season with Minnesota before retiring (for good).

5. Randall Cunningham

What a season 1998 was for the Vikings! Following an excellent 11-year run with the Philadelphia Eagles, during which he was a three-time Pro Bowler, Cunningham had one of the greatest seasons in NFL history for the 15–1 Vikings. He appeared in just 27 games for Minnesota over three seasons.

6. Jack Morris

Another St. Paul product (Highland Park High School), Jack came home to Minnesota in 1991 after 14 years with the Detroit Tigers. During his brief stopover, he capped off an All-Star season by pitching one of the greatest games in World Series history, a 1–0, ten-inning shutout in the seventh game of the 1991 series to clinch the Twins' second championship. Jack also came out of retirement in 1996 at age 41 to play for the independent minor league St. Paul Saints, for whom he went 5–1 with a 2.69 ERA.

7. Warren Moon

A great quarterback with the Houston Oilers and the Edmonton Eskimos of the Canadian Football League, Moon had a brief stint with the Vikings from 1994 to 1996 and lit up the field. He is one of only a few players to be inducted in both the Pro Football Hall of Fame in Canton, Ohio, and the Canadian Football Hall of Fame in Hamilton, Ontario.

8. Herschel Walker

Although mention of his name will make many Minnesota fans cringe because of the disastrous trade that brought him here, Herschel was one of the biggest names in pro sports when he joined the Vikings in 1989. He had been a big star at Georgia and then with the Cowboys before his star flamed out in Minnesota.

9. Elmer "Moose" Vasko

"Moose" played out the final years of his NHL career with the North Stars after establishing himself as a big, powerful defenseman with Chicago, where he was known for guarding the blue line and the net. He played 11 years with the Blackhawks and captained the North Stars during his two seasons here.

10. Roger Craig

Craig is best known as the star running back for the three-time Super Bowl champion San Francisco 49ers of the 1980s, but he had a "cup of coffee" with the Vikings in 1992 and 1993 before hanging up the cleats.

10 ATHLETES MOST HATED BY MINNESOTA FANS

Local fans have been known to forego "Minnesota nice" when it comes to their favorite sports teams. Sometimes the hatred was cultivated by many years of competing against the hometown team, and in some cases all it took was a single incident to incur the wrath of the Minnesota faithful—and sometimes the disdain was directed at players wearing home uniforms.

1. Drew Pearson

The Dallas Cowboys wide receiver takes first place for his infamous, non-called, push-off of Vikings defensive back Nate Wright in the 1975 divisional playoff game at Metropolitan Stadium. The flagrant act cost the Vikings a trip to the Super Bowl and ended the season for one of the best Vikings teams ever.

2. Gary Anderson

Anderson had been fantastic all year long for the Vikings in 1998, not missing a single field goal or extra point during the entire regular season. But when he did finally miss—a 38-yard field goal attempt in the waning minutes of the NFC Championship Game against the Atlanta Falcons—it cost Minnesota a trip to the Super Bowl. It was another heartbreaking loss for Vikings fans, bringing to an end what had been a magical 15–1 season. Many will never forgive him.

3. Brett Favre

A lot of Vikings fans may have proudly donned Favre jerseys in 2009 and 2010 during Brett's two seasons with the Vikings, but for most Minnesota sports fans, he will always be remembered—and despised—for his long tenure as quarterback of the hated Green Bay Packers.

4. Chuck Knoblauch

Although the fiery second baseman had a good career in Minnesota—including American League Rookie of the Year honors in 1991 and four All-Star appearances in seven seasons with the Twins—he got on the fans' bad side once he demanded to be traded. After he was sent to the New York Yankees before the 1998 season, he was treated to much abuse and heckling from the Twins faithful. On one occasion—"Dollar Dog Day" in 2001—he was pelted by hot dogs, plastic bottles, and other debris when he took his position in the outfield. The game was delayed twice, and Twins manager Tom Kelly had to walk out to the area in front of the stands to ask the fans to stop throwing objects on the field.

5. Maurice "Mad Dog" Vachon

The "Mad Dog" will always go down as one of the most despised and hated wrestlers of all time. After all, he was the rival of a hometown hero, Vern Gagne, in the American Wrestling Association during the 1960s. He made his name in the AWA for his vicious, rule-breaking tactics.

6. Dick Butkus

Butkus was disliked mostly because he played middle linebacker for the hated Monsters of the Midway, the Chicago Bears, in the late 1960s and early '70s. The fact that he was such a great player didn't exactly help his popularity among the Minnesota faithful. Butkus revolutionized the middle linebacker position in pro football.

(Continued)

7. A. J. Pierzynski

We loved him when he was a Twin, and we loved how the opposing teams and fans hated him. But when he signed with the rival White Sox in 2005, the tables were turned, and he was roundly booed and harassed whenever he came back to Minnesota to play. I don't know what it is about A. J., but he seems to bring about the worst in himself for fans to hate.

8. Mike Ditka

Another Hall of Famer who played for the Chicago Bears, Ditka was one of the greatest tight ends to ever play the game. His unpopularity really skyrocketed among Minnesotans when he was the coach of the Bears from 1982 to 1992.

9. Randy Moss

Moss managed to generate plenty of controversy during his first tenure with the Vikings (1998–2004), but it was during his second time around that he did just about everything he could to alienate himself from the fans. His second stay didn't last long—only four games in the middle of the 2010 season—but it was a reunion most Vikings fans would prefer to forget, and it overrode a lot of the fond memories of his great on-field accomplishments during his first go-round. His last stop here sealed the deal with an incident in the Vikings cafeteria with a food vendor. Too bad; he was one of the greatest ever!

10. John Bailey and Cy Whiteside

We have to go back to the 1950s and 1960s and the great International Hockey League rivalry between the St. Paul Fighting Saints and the Minneapolis Millers to revive these two players. Depending on the side of the river you came from determined which one you hated. Bailey was a right winger for the Saints from 1959 to 1962, and Whiteside was a Millers defenseman from '59 to '63. When the two went head-to-head on the ice, it was really something to see.

10 GREATEST MINNESOTA SPORTS RIVALS

It's hard to keep the blood from boiling just thinking about these rivalries. Whenever these teams come to town, the anticipation is as dramatic and exciting as it gets.

1. Green Bay Packers

Whenever the Vikes take on the rivals from the state next door, it is simply called "Packer week." There is no team anywhere or at any time that I would rather see us beat than the Green Bay Packers! Bud Grant's first victory as Vikings head coach came against Vince Lombardi's Packers. Over the years, the teams' respective fortunes have not always aligned, and the rivals have met only twice in the playoffs—in 2004, when the Vikes came out on top 31–17 in a wild card game, and in 2012, when the Pack got its revenge with a 24–10 win, just six days after Minnesota beat them in the regular-season finale to clinch a playoff spot. Overall, the Packers hold a 54–48 advantage (through 2013) in regular-season meetings.

2. Chicago Bears

The Bears are a close second to the Packers in teams we want to see lose at any cost. In the first game in Vikings franchise history, rookie quarterback Fran Tarkenton came off the bench and threw four touchdown passes and ran for another to lead the upstart Vikings to a 37–13 win over the vaunted Monsters of the Midway—one of the greatest upsets in NFL history. Since then, the Vikes have come out on top in 52 regular-season games, while the Bears have bested Minnesota 49 times plus once in the postseason. And even though my friend Marc Trestman is now the head coach in Chicago, I still want the Bears to lose!

(Continued)

3. Chicago White Sox

Another Chicago team that Minnesota fans love to hate. For years, it seemed like it was always the Twins and Sox battling for the division crown. During the six seasons that the Twins won the Central Division from 2002 to 2010, Chicago finished in second place four times, and the Sox won two division titles of their own during that stretch, including 2008, when they defeated the Twins in a one-game playoff to decide the division. With A. J. Pierzynski behind the plate and the outspoken Ozzie Guillen managing the team, the rivalry's intensity was particularly high.

4. Wisconsin Badgers

Whether on the gridiron or on the ice, it is always gratifying to see the Gophers beat the Badgers. Although the Badgers football team has seen greater success in recent years (three straight Big Ten titles from 2010 to 2012), the Gophers hold the advantage in their head-to-head meetings (59–55–8) dating back to 1890. Since 1948, the winner of the game has taken home the prized Paul Bunyan's Axe, with the game results inscribed on the handle. The Gophers' all-time edge over the Badgers in hockey is much greater, but the "Border Battle" rivalry is no less intense whenever the teams meet at Mariucci Arena or at the Kohl Center in Madison.

5. Michigan Wolverines

Nearly as long as the Gophers–Badgers football rivalry is the one between the Gophers and the Wolverines. Unfortunately, the results have been so one-sided in Michigan's favor, and the "Little Brown Jug" trophy has been awarded to the Gophers only 24 times compared to 73 for the Wolverines since their first meeting in 1892 (although the jug wasn't introduced as a trophy until 1903). Still, there have been some great matchups over the years. In 1940, the undefeated Gophers beat the undefeated Wolverines en route to a Big Ten title. In 1977 and again in 1986, Minnesota handed

Michigan its only losses of those seasons. A memorable game that Gophers fans would prefer to forget was in 2003, when Michigan scored 21 fourth-quarter points to come from behind to beat the Gophers 38–35. By the way, I hate their uniforms too!

6. Iowa Hawkeyes

This rivalry with yet another Big Ten foe is nearly in the Michigan and Wisconsin category. The teams first met in 1891, and Minnesota has won 61 times overall compared to 44 for Iowa (with two ties). Since 1935, the Floyd of Rosedale trophy—a bronze pig—is awarded to the winner. Back in 1960, the third-ranked Gophers went into Iowa's Memorial Stadium and defeated the top-ranked Hawkeyes 27–10; both teams were undefeated at that point, and the win helped secure the Big Ten title and the national championship for Minnesota.

7. Chicago Blackhawks

Now that the NHL has realigned its divisions, and the Minnesota and Chicago clubs are in the same division, the hatred for the Blackhawks will once again intensify. I mean, it's Chicago and we already hate the Bears and White Sox, so why not include the Blackhawks too? Of course, there were some great battles back in the day at the Met Center between the Hawks and the North Stars.

8. St. Paul Fighting Saints vs. Minneapolis Millers Hockey

This goes back a few years, but the rivalry between these two minor league hockey teams and their fans was pretty intense. The clubs were part of the International Hockey Association from 1959 to 1963, and the games between the two often featured brawls on the ice and in the stands. Things got pretty wild at the old St. Paul Auditorium and the Minneapolis Arena on Dupont. (There had been Millers and Saints teams in the old American Hockey Association and the U.S. Hockey Association as well, going back to the 1920s.)

(Continued)

9. St. Paul Saints vs. Minneapolis Millers Baseball

Though perhaps not as intense as their hockey rivalry, the Saints–Millers rivalry in baseball's old American Association spanned six decades (1902–60). From the late 1940s until 1957, the Saints were an affiliate of the Brooklyn Dodgers while the Millers were affiliated with the New York Giants, adding to the intrigue. For decades, every Fourth of July, the teams would play a doubleheader, with one game played at Minneapolis' Nicollet Park and the other played at St. Paul's Lexington Park, as fans rode the trolleys between the cities. Those were the days!

10. North Dakota Fighting Sioux

The Gophers men's hockey team first took on the Fighting Sioux on the ice in 1930, and you can feel the intensity of this rivalry the minute you walk into Mariucci Arena or Grand Forks' Ralph Engelstad Arena any time the teams go head-to-head. The players feel it too, and fights have been known to break out between the teams, even during post-game handshake lines! Minnesota holds a 146–130–15 edge in head-to-head meetings overall, although with the Gophers' move to the Big Ten and UND's move to the NCHC, the rivalry has faded.

10 BIGGEST MINNESOTA SPORTS BUSTS

Sometimes when players and coaches come to Minnesota with much anticipation and promise, things don't quite turn out as we would've hoped. Here are some of the bigger disappointments endured by Minnesota sports fans over the years.

1. Herschel Walker

The 1989 trade with Dallas goes down as one of the worst ever in professional sports. Herschel never lived up to expectations after coming over from Dallas in a trade for five players and nine draft choices. That's right: 14 players! Herschel had been a great college star at Georgia and was coming off back-to-back Pro Bowl seasons with the Cowboys, but after an incredible first game in Minnesota (148 yards rushing against the Packers), he was little more than a mediocre back for the next two and a half seasons. Meanwhile, the players and draft picks the Vikings gave up helped turn the Cowboys into a perennial contender. It took the Vikings many years to recover.

2. Tommy Herr

This was one of the worst trades the Twins ever made, as they gave up 27-year-old slugger Tom Brunansky for a middle infielder in the waning years of his career. Not only was Herr a bad player for the Twins, but by everyone's account, he wasn't a very nice person either. The trade seemed to make little sense, particularly coming so soon on the heels of the 1987 World Series win.

3. Tsuyoshi Nishioka

In 2011, the Twins bid $5 million for the right to sign Nishioka, who had established himself as a major star with Japan's Chiba Lotte Marines. The Twins were looking for an everyday player to fill their middle-infield void. It didn't work—in startling fashion. Nishioka simply couldn't hit big-league pitching, posting a .215 average in one season before returning to Japan.

(Continued)

4. Les Steckel

One of the biggest busts as a head coach ever. Les had been an up-and-comer as an assistant on Bud Grant's staff. When Grant retired, Steckel, who was a favorite of General Manager Mike Lynn, was chosen to fill Grant's shoes. The Vikings believed that Steckel would follow in Grant's footsteps as a young head coach who would hold the job for a long time to come. Steckel's 3–13 record in 1984 brought a quick end to his Vikings career.

5. Tim Brewster

Some say he was overmatched by Big Ten football—and they're probably correct. Coming off five seasons as a tight-ends coach in the NFL and, before that, 13 seasons as a college assistant, Brewster came in with a lot of hype and left with a pretty bad record: 15–30 overall and 6–21 in the conference.

6. Lou Holtz

Lou makes this list not because he didn't do a fantastic job as coach of the Gophers but because he left for Notre Dame just when things were getting good. It devastated Gophers fans when he said goodbye after only two seasons. The stadium was full and the fans were sniffing roses, and then Lou left. No one except the U of M administration knew of the out-clause in Holtz's contract relating to any offer from Notre Dame. The offer came, and Lou was gone.

7. Jerry Shay

Shay, a defensive lineman out of Purdue, was a first-round draft pick (number seven overall) for the Vikings in 1966. The giant, 250-pound tackle was expected to have an immediate impact. Instead, he appeared in only 15 games for Minnesota before going to Atlanta and then the Giants. He was out of the league by the time he was 27.

8. Archie Sutton

Another high draft choice by the Vikings who never came through as expected. Sutton was an offensive lineman with a great collegiate career behind him at Illinois. The Vikings picked him in the second round of the 1965 draft, and he was gone after 19 career games in the NFL.

9. Leo Hayden

Hayden was a big running back from Ohio State who was taken by the Vikings in the first round of the 1971 draft. He did not have a single rushing carry for the Vikings during his very brief stay.

10. Eddie Bane

Eddie was believed to be a sure-thing pitcher when he was taken as a first-round selection out of Arizona State by the Twins in the 1973 draft. After going 0–5 with a 4.92 ERA in his rookie year, he spent nearly all of the next two seasons in the minor leagues. He did win three of the four games he started for the Twins in 1975, but after a 4–7 campaign in 1976, he was out of the majors for good, winner of only seven games in his major league career.

5 WORST TRADES IN MINNESOTA SPORTS

1. **Trade for Herschel Walker from the Dallas Cowboys**
When the Vikings first made this 1989 trade, it looked pretty good. Once it became clear that Walker was not going to work out as anticipated, the five players and nine high draft picks the Vikings gave up crippled the team for many seasons. The trade vaulted Dallas into championship contention.

2. **Trade for Tommy Herr from the St. Louis Cardinals**
It was hard for Twins fan to believe that popular Tom Brunansky was traded to St. Louis for second baseman Tommy Herr after the 1987 World Series. Herr never worked out here as a player and was about as unpopular a player as the Twins have ever had. It was a horrible trade.

3. **Trading Nick Leddy to the Chicago Blackhawks**
Leddy was the first-round draft choice of the Minnesota Wild in 2009 when he was playing for the Gophers. In 2010, before he even suited up for the Wild, he was traded with Kim Johnson to the Blackhawks for Cam Barker. Leddy is now playing extremely well for Chicago, while Barker is no longer with the Wild.

4. **Trading Kevin Garnett to the Boston Celtics**
The face of the Timberwolves franchise was traded to the Boston Celtics in 2007. It was a huge trade at the time, as Garnett had been with the Wolves ever since he was their number one draft choice in 1995. Although they acquired up-and-coming big man Al Jefferson along with four other players and two draft picks, the Wolves didn't get anyone to fill Garnett's shoes as a player and a leader until Kevin Love came along.

5. **Trading Johan Santana to the New York Mets**
The Twins' trade of star pitcher and former Cy Young Award winner Johan Santana in 2008 for four players was a total bust. None of the four made any impact for the Twins and none remains on the roster.

10 BIGGEST MINNESOTA SPORTS SCANDALS AND CONTROVERSIES

Unfortunately, we have had our share of big stories and incidents that have rocked our sports world right here in Minnesota.

1. Norm Green Moves the North Stars to Dallas in 1993
There were significant financial reasons and other issues behind why the move was made, but the bottom line was that our beloved Minnesota North Stars were gone and the NHL was no longer in the Twin Cities.

2. Minnesota Gophers–Ohio State Buckeyes brawl at Williams Arena in 1972
With 36 seconds left in the game, Ohio State center Luke Witte was fouled and knocked to the floor by Gopher Corky Taylor. Taylor extended his hand to help Witte up and then proceeded to knee him in the groin and punch him. The brawl was on, one of the ugliest in collegiate sports history. Athletic Director Paul Giel forfeited the game with the Gophers trailing by six points.

3. Gophers Basketball Academic Fraud Scandal
It was bad enough that all postseason records from 1993 to 1998 have been officially erased from the NCAA records. It was an embarrassing time for Minnesota basketball.

4. Near-Contraction of the Twins in 2002
The Minnesota Twins were almost no more in 2002 when owner Carl Pohlad had discussions with MLB Commissioner Bud Selig about possibly eliminating the team from Major League Baseball due to its financial struggles. Although it never came to fruition, just the idea of the behind-the-back scheming is almost too much to consider, even more than a decade later.

(Continued)

5. Calvin Griffith's Racist Comments during a Speech

At a Lions Club dinner in Waseca, Minnesota, in 1978, Twins owner Calvin made some outlandish racist remarks relating to why he moved the team from Washington, D.C., to Minnesota. The comments soiled his legacy as owner of the Minnesota Twins forever.

6. Randy Moss Incidents

He had multiple incidents that made the headlines. Randy was fined by the NFL in 2000 for squirting a game official with a water bottle, and he was fined by the league again for pretending to moon the Green Bay fans after a touchdown during the 2004 playoffs. In between, in 2002, he was arrested and sentenced to pay a fine and perform community service after almost running over a traffic officer with his vehicle. And then there was the incident with the food vendor at Winter Park during his second time with the Vikings.

7. The Joe Smith Contract

Following the 1999–2000 season, it was learned that the Timberwolves had manipulated the contract of forward Joe Smith in order to open salary room. It resulted in the team losing five first-round draft picks, although two were later returned to the Timberwolves.

8. **Kirby Puckett's Alleged Assault of a Woman at a Local Restaurant**

Just mentioning the beloved former Twin in anything bad was upsetting to his many fans and the sports world. No one ever wanted to hear anything bad about Kirby. This 2002 incident made headline news.

9. **The Dennis Green Knee**

Coach Green's infamous decision to have Randall Cunningham take a knee rather than make another try for the end zone in the final seconds of regulation during the 1998 NFC Championship Game will always be a dark moment in Vikings history. Minnesota had the most explosive offense in NFL history, and fans could not understand why the Vikings did not go for a score to try to break the 27–27 tie, rather than just let the game go into overtime. And of course, the Vikings went on to lose the game in overtime.

10. **Joe Niekro's Emery Board**

Maybe it's not so scandalous, but it sure was an unusual moment when umpire Tim Tschida caught Joe Niekro, a notorious scuff-ball pitcher, with an emery board in his pocket. An emery board to doctor a baseball? Never. It cost Joe a ten-game suspension in 1987.

MEMORABLE BUT DEFUNCT MINNESOTA TEAMS

We have had some great memories of professional teams in the Twin Cities. Unfortunately, a good number of them are no longer in existence. The rankings here are not in any particular order.

1. Minnesota Muskies

A charter member of the American Basketball Association (ABA), the Muskies operated in the Twin Cities for the 1967–68 season before moving to Miami to become the Floridians. Coached by former Minneapolis Laker and Hall of Fame player Jim Pollard, the Muskies reached the playoffs in their lone season with a 50–28 record.

2. Minnesota Pipers

Another ABA team in the Twin Cities that lasted only a short time, the Pipers moved from Pittsburgh before the 1968–69 season and then returned to Pittsburgh after just one campaign in Minnesota. Basketball Hall of Famer Connie Hawkins donned the Pipers uniform during the team's one season in Minnesota, and former Minneapolis Lakers legend Vern Mikkelsen was the general manager.

3. Minnesota North Stars

The North Stars were one of the all-time favorite teams among Minnesota fans, and it was devastating to the area when they moved to Dallas. The team operated here from 1967 to 1993.

4. Minnesota Fighting Saints

The Fighting Saints of the World Hockey Association were in operation for five seasons, playing their home games at the St. Paul Civic Center. The original team lasted from 1972 to 1976 before ceasing operations, and a second incarnation came along for the 1976–77 season before that version folded.

5. Minnesota Kicks

A professional team in the North American Soccer League, the Kicks operated here from 1976 to 1981. Playing most of their games at Met Stadium in Bloomington, the Kicks reached the NASL Soccer Bowl in their inaugural season but lost the championship game.

6. Minnesota Strikers

Another professional soccer team, the Strikers played in the North American Soccer League in 1984 and then shifted to the Major Indoor Soccer League, where they remained until 1988. They moved to Minnesota from Fort Lauderdale, Florida, in 1984.

7. Minneapolis Millers

Several local minor league baseball teams carried the name of the Minneapolis Millers in the 19th century, but the longtime American Association club played here from 1902 to 1960. At times during their existence, the Millers served as the minor league affiliate of the Boston Red Sox and New York Giants, and such legends as Ted Williams, Willie Mays, and Carl Yastrzemski, among others, played for the Millers at Nicollet Park in Minneapolis or Met Stadium in Bloomington.

8. St. Paul Saints

No, not the current team of the independent Northern League that plays at Midway Stadium. The original baseball Saints were another team from the American Association and longtime rivals of the Millers. Playing at Lexington Park and then Midway Stadium from 1901 to 1960, the Saints were affiliates of the White Sox and Dodgers, during which time baseball Hall of Famer Roy Campanella played here.

9. Minneapolis Lakers

It is hard to believe that the famous Los Angeles Lakers franchise of NBA fame was our own Minneapolis Lakers from 1947 to 1960. Led by the great George Mikan, the Lakers won five NBA championships in Minneapolis before leaving for Los Angeles in 1960.

10. Duluth Eskimos

Going away from the Twin Cities for a moment, Duluth was home to a professional football team in the 1920s. Founded as the Duluth Kelleys in 1923 in the early years of the NFL, the team became the Eskimos in 1926 before folding after the 1927 season. These Pro Football Hall of Famers spent time with the Eskimos: Walt Kiesling, John "Blood" McNally, and Ernie Nevers.

GREATEST MINNESOTA TWINS HITTER · BIGGEST
ESOTA VIKINGS HEARTBREAK · HERB BROOKS
ESOTA'S GREATEST HOCKEY LEGEND · MOST M
ABLE RANDY MOSS MOMENTS · LINDSEY WH
GREATEST MINNESOTA TIMBERWOLVES MOM
JOE MAUER · BEST DRAFT DECISION · MOS
ARRE TWINS INJURY · TONY OLIVA · MINNES
EST SPORTS BARS · BEST BALLPARK GRUB ·

FOOTBALL

OST SURPRISING BREAK-OUT STAR · PATTY
NEAL BROTEN · BIGGEST SPORTS BUST ·
N GABORIK · MOST DRAMATIC GOPHER VICT
EN BEST THINGS ABOUT "THE BARN" · ROD CA
ARMON KILLEBREW · GEORGE MIKAN · KEVIN
TT · RICKY RUBIO · CLASSIC AMERICAN WRES
SSOCIATION MOMENTS · HARMON KILLEB
RAN TARKENTON · PURPLE PEOPLE EATERS

10 GREATEST MINNESOTA VIKINGS MOMENTS

1. First Vikings Game Ever

September 17, 1961, may go down as the day of one of the greatest upsets in NFL history. An upstart collection of rookies and castoffs from other teams defeated the mighty Monsters of the Midway in the Minnesota Vikings' inaugural game at old Metropolitan Stadium. A young rookie quarterback by the name of Francis Asbury Tarkenton came off the bench to throw four touchdown passes and run for another as the Vikings won the game 37-13.

2. Drafting Fran Tarkenton

When Minnesota selected the University of Georgia quarterback with their third-round pick in 1961, no one knew at the time that the Vikings had gotten their hands on a future Hall of Famer. Fran proved his worth by becoming one of the most exciting quarterbacks in the history of the game, eventually leading the Vikings to three Super Bowls during his second tenure with the team.

3. Tommy Kramer's Pass to Ahmad Rashad to Defeat Cleveland in 1980

"Five seconds left, Kramer back to pass. . . . He is going deep down the right side . . . Rashad! Touchdown!!" The immortal words of announcer Ray Scott described Tommy Kramer hitting Ahmad Rashad down the right sideline for a 46-yard touchdown to defeat the Cleveland Browns on the last play to send the Vikings to the playoffs. Kramer threw for 456 yards and four touchdowns in the game, with Rashad on the receiving end of 142 of those yards and two of the touchdowns.

4. Victory over Cleveland in 1969 NFL Championship Game

Just a week after defeating a great Rams team, the Vikings took on the Cleveland Browns for the NFL championship and the right to play in the fourth Super Bowl. With the temperature at eight degrees and the wind chill at minus-six at the Met, Minnesota jumped out to a

(Continued)

24–0 lead in the first half before cruising to a 27–7 final. Quarterback Joe Kapp hit receiver Gene Washington on a 75-yard pass play for a first-quarter touchdown, and Dave Osborn gained 108 yards rushing in the game, while Minnesota's Purple People Eaters defense held the Cleveland offense in check. The Vikings were on their way to take on the Kansas City Chiefs in their first Super Bowl.

5. 1973 NFC Championship Game against the Dallas Cowboys

Despite finishing the 1973 season with a 12–2 record, the Vikings headed to Dallas as heavy underdogs in their conference championship meeting with the Cowboys. Behind another great defensive performance and a tremendous offensive game plan put together by offensive coordinator Jerry Burns and executed by Fran Tarkenton and the Vikings offense, Minnesota came out victorious, 27–10. Chuck Foreman and Oscar Reed led a rushing attack that gained more than 200 yards, and a pair of interceptions by Bobby Bryant contributed to six turnovers by the Cowboys. The win, one of the greatest in franchise history, sent the Purple to their second Super Bowl.

6. Alan Page Wins MVP Award in 1971

A defensive lineman had never won the Most Valuable Player Award in the National Football League—not until Alan Page came along. Alan had a tremendous season leading the Purple People Eaters as one of the most dominating defenses in all of professional football during the Vikings' 11–3 campaign in 1971. Page was an unstoppable force on the defensive line—quick, agile, and a tremendous pass rusher. His dominance on the line for the Vikings was among the best every year that he played, but 1971 was voted as his best.

7. 1969 Playoff Win against the Los Angeles Rams

Capping off a 12–2 regular season, the Vikings' come-from-behind playoff victory over the Rams was a signature game for Bud Grant's team. Just three weeks after defeating the then-undefeated Rams in Los Angeles, the Vikings played host for the opening round of the playoffs at cold and snowy Metropolitan Stadium. Trailing 20–14 in the fourth quarter, Joe Kapp marched the team down the field for a touchdown and a 21–20 advantage. A Carl Eller sack of L.A. quarterback Roman Gabriel in the end zone made it 23–20, and then Alan Page's interception in the Rams' final drive clinched it for the Purple. The dramatic win helped vault the team into its peak glory years.

8. Randy Moss vs. Packers in 1998

In his first game against Green Bay as a member of the Vikings, Randy Moss reeled in 190 yards receiving and two touchdowns as Minnesota defeated the defending NFC champion Packers at Lambeau Field—and it was on national television! It was one of the most dominating performances by a wide receiver, and it led Green Bay to change its draft strategy regarding defensive backs.

9. Brett Favre Arrives in the Twin Cities

Love him or hate him, Brett Favre arriving in the Twin Cities as a Minnesota Viking will go down as a great moment for the franchise. Favre had an incredible first season with the Vikings (4,202 yards and 33 touchdowns), and he led them to within one game of the Super Bowl.

10. Hiring Bud Grant as Vikings Head Coach

Maybe this should be number one on the list. Before he was hired by the Vikings in 1967, Bud had been a successful coach in the Canadian Football League, winning four Grey Cups with the Winnipeg Blue Bombers. He brought that winning tradition with him to Minnesota and became one of the greatest coaches in the history of the NFL. In 1993, he was elected to the Pro Football Hall of Fame.

10 WORST MINNESOTA VIKINGS MOMENTS

1. Four Super Bowl Losses

They were all painful following great seasons for the Vikings. First it was Kansas City following the 1969 season. Then it was Miami after the 1973 season, followed by Pittsburgh the very next year, and finally Oakland after the 1976 season.

2. Les Steckel's Season in 1984

This has to go down as a low point in Vikings history. Les Steckel took a reasonably competitive team and in one short season turned it into a 3–13 team. He lasted only one year, and Bud Grant was brought back to restore order in the franchise before Jerry Burns took over. It wasn't just the one bad season led by Steckel. Under Bud Grant, the fan base always believed in the coach and the team and knew that he could turn the team around even after a few bad seasons. With Steckel, everything the Vikings stood for seemed to collapse, with little hope for the future. The rock-solid base that Grant had established crumbled, and the faithful regained hope only with the announcement that Bud was returning the next year.

3. Herschel Walker Trade

When the trade was first announced, fans thought this blockbuster was going to bring years of success. The team gave up a total of 14 players, nine of them significant draft picks, to the Dallas Cowboys. The trade vaulted Dallas into playoff prominence for many seasons while holding the Vikings in recovery mode. It has gone down in history as one of the worst trades ever.

4. The 1975 Dallas Playoff Game

Those who saw this debacle will never forget it. I sure won't! A non-call for what was clearly offensive pass interference by Drew Pearson knocked the Vikings out of the playoffs and ended the season for what many would call the greatest team in franchise history. Roger Staubach to Drew Pearson for the touchdown will haunt Vikings fans forever.

5. Gary Anderson Missed Field Goal

Kicker Anderson had a storybook season until he missed on a 38-yard field goal in the 1998 NFC Championship Game against the Atlanta Falcons—his only miss of any kick all season. It ultimately cost the Purple the chance to go to the Super Bowl and ended the run by one of the highest scoring and most productive offensive teams in NFL history.

6. The Dennis Green Knee

Same game, same team as number 5 above. With the score tied and the Vikings getting control of the ball in the final minute, head coach Dennis Green chose to have quarterback Randall Cunningham take a knee and let the clock run out, thus forcing overtime, rather than taking a shot at the end zone with another attempt down the field. (The Vikings had two timeouts left at the time.) Fans will never forgive him.

(Continued)

7. Bud Grant's Retirements

No one, and I mean no one, could believe that Bud Grant would retire as head coach of the Vikings. But he did just that following the 1983 season, after 17 seasons at the helm. I covered the story from Hawaii, and later, after the official announcement, I had Bud, new head coach Les Steckel, and several other Vikings on Rosen Sports Sunday. It was tough enough losing Bud the first time, but after he came back to coach in 1985, his second retirement hit Vikings fans hard once again. This time, however, it was softened a little when his replacement was announced to be Jerry Burns. Jerry did an excellent job following Bud for the five years he stayed as head coach.

8. 41–Donut

Just two years removed from the heartbreaking loss to the Falcons in the 1998 NFC Championship Game, the Vikings returned to the conference title game, traveling to the Meadowlands to face the New York Giants on January 14, 2001. The 11–5 Vikings had won their division, but the 41–0 humiliation at the hands of the Giants brought the season to an ugly conclusion. The vaunted Minnesota offense managed to gain only 114 total yards in the game while the Kerry Collins–led Giants cruised to 518 yards of offense.

9. The Favre Interception

After an incredible season in which the aging but effective Brett Favre led Minnesota to a 12–4 record and a division title, the Vikings played New Orleans in the Superdome for the NFC championship in January 2010. An errant pass by Favre late in the game, along with a penalty for too many men in the huddle, cost the Vikings another trip to the Super Bowl.

10. Adrian Peterson's Injury

When Adrian Peterson tore up his knee at the end of the 2011 season, it was a tense and uncertain year as we wondered if he could recover. And he sure did! We would never have guessed that he would come back so strong the following season and almost set the NFL season rushing record. He set a new standard for his position and gave hope to others in the recovery process from knee injuries.

MINNESOTA VIKINGS ALL-TIME OFFENSIVE LINEUP

I love doing this list because these all-time great players bring back so many memories from throughout the decades of Vikings history. It's a shame they could not have all been in their primes at the same time. Imagine how many Super Bowls they would have won!

Center: Mick Tingelhoff
Mick played center for the Vikings for 17 seasons and started more than 260 consecutive games. He was the long snapper and was also noted for his downfield tackles on interceptions and punt returns.

Guard: Randall McDaniel
Randall was one of the most powerful and explosive guards to ever play the game. An 11-time Pro Bowler and seven-time All-Pro in 12 seasons with the Purple, he was inducted into the Pro Football Hall of Fame in 2009.

Guard: Ed White
Ed was one of the strongest players to ever play for Minnesota. He won several national arm wrestling contests and was a mainstay for the Vikings during their glory years (1969–77).

Tackle: Ron Yary
Hall of Famer Ron Yary was a dominating tackle for the Vikings from 1968 to 1981, during which time he was named a First Team All-Pro in six consecutive seasons (1971–76). Bud Grant used to say that he didn't care if defenders knew they were going to run a play behind Yary, because even if they defended it, the Vikings would still get the yardage they needed.

Tackle: Grady Alderman

Grady joined the Vikings in the inaugural season of 1961 and stayed with the team through 1974. He was an outstanding pass blocker, and he stabilized everything on the right side of the line.

Tight End: Steve Jordan

Steve was as solid a football player as you could find. He was strong and could run, catch passes, and block. The Vikings have had some outstanding tight ends in their 50-plus years, and Steve Jordan ranks at the top.

Wide Receiver: Cris Carter

After a long wait, Cris finally was elected to the Pro Football Hall of Fame in 2013; he should have gotten in during his first year of eligibility. All he did was catch touchdown passes (paraphrasing his former Eagles coach Buddy Ryan) and make some incredible plays throughout his career. He spent 12 seasons in Minnesota and holds the franchise records for receptions, yards, and touchdowns. Simply one of the greatest wide receivers of all time.

Wide Receiver: Randy Moss

Even though there always seemed to be some kind of crazy sideline or off-the-field controversy surrounding him, Randy was unquestionably one of the most exciting wide receivers to ever play the game. His early years with the Vikings were absolutely phenomenal, as he made five Pro Bowls in seven seasons and led the league in receiving TDs three times.

(Continued)

Quarterback: Fran Tarkenton

Known as "The Scrambler," Tarkenton was one of football's most exciting and prolific quarterbacks. He led the Vikings to three Super Bowls and spent 13 years in Minnesota. The Hall of Famer is the franchise's all-time leader in nearly every passing category, including attempts, completions, yardage, touchdowns, and wins.

Running Back: Adrian Peterson

Although he hasn't played that many years to this point, it's impossible to leave him off the list. Peterson is on his way to possibly becoming the greatest running back of all time. After six years in the league, he had already catapulted to the top of the list in most Vikings rushing categories, and he was named a First Team All-Pro in three of those six seasons. By the time he's done, he'll likely hold many NFL records for running backs.

Running Back: Bill "Boom Boom" Brown

There may have been running backs that could do a few things better than Bill, but no one has better captured the heart and soul of Vikings football than "Boom Boom" Brown. He played here from 1962 to 1974, and he could run the ball, catch the ball, and throw a ferocious block.

Kicker: Fred Cox

This is an easy one. Fred is the Vikings' all-time leading scorer. He was consistent and contributed to the team in so many ways for 15 seasons (1963–77).

MINNESOTA VIKINGS ALL-TIME DEFENSIVE LINEUP

Defensive End: Jim Marshall
There can never be an All-Vikings anything without Jim Marshall. A member of the legendary Purple People Eaters defensive line, Jim started 282 consecutive games and always played at an incredibly high level. Vikings football and Jim Marshall are one in the same! It's really a shame that he has not been honored at the Pro Football Hall of Fame.

Defensive End: Carl Eller
There is no doubt that Jared Allen will someday be recognized as one of the greatest defensive ends in NFL history, but at this time Carl Eller is cemented in on my list. After having the privilege of watching Carl play at the University of Minnesota, we got to watch him as a member of the Vikings for 15 seasons. Another of the Purple People Eaters, Carl was inducted into the Pro Football Hall of Fame in 2004.

Defensive Tackle: Alan Page
Alan was the first defensive lineman to win the NFL MVP Award—an amazing feat!—and was elected to the Pro Bowl in nine consecutive seasons. A Pro Football Hall of Famer, Page had the ability to take over a football game, and at times in key situations he was virtually unstoppable. He will go down as one of the best tackles to ever play pro football.

Defensive Tackle: John Randle
How does a player go undrafted and make it into the Pro Football Hall of Fame? John Randle did it and in fiery fashion as a tremendous player on the Vikings' defensive line from 1990 to 2000. A six-time All-Pro, John played the game with ferocity, and he ranks as the franchise's all-time leader in quarterback sacks. (Sacks were not an official statistic during the days of the Purple People Eaters.)

(Continued)

Linebacker: Scott Studwell

Scott was a star linebacker for the Vikings from 1977 to 1990. He still holds the record for the most tackles for any one team in NFL history, with 1,981. He also holds team records for single-season tackles with 230 in 1981, as well the team's single-game record, with 24 in a game against Detroit in 1985. The durable Studwell, mostly playing the middle or inside linebacker positions, was a tackling machine for the Purple.

Linebacker: Matt Blair

Another career Viking, Matt Blair was outstanding in all aspects of the game. He blocked more kicks for Minnesota (22.5) than most teams block in decades, and he ranks first among Vikings linebackers in career interceptions. He was a tremendous defender and a mainstay at the position, earning six straight Pro Bowl nods from 1977 to 1982.

Linebacker: Jeff Siemon

A native of Rochester, Minnesota, Jeff was a terrific middle linebacker for the Vikings throughout the 1970s. He was tough and could really move around on the defense. He started at the position and excelled for many seasons, establishing himself as one of the Vikings' best defensive players of all time.

Cornerback: Bobby Bryant

Bobby was a key member of the Vikings' defensive backfield during the Bud Grant era, playing from 1968 to 1980. Fast, strong, and able to really cover the field, Bryant made some incredible big plays at key times in key games. He ranks second to Paul Krause on the all-time franchise list for interceptions, with 51 picks.

Cornerback: Carl Lee

Carl was a solid defensive back for the Vikings from 1983 to 1993 and has always been recognized as one of the best players the team has ever had in the defensive backfield. During his All-Pro season of 1988, he ran two interceptions back for touchdowns.

Safety: Paul Krause

Paul was one of the greatest defensive backs to ever play in the NFL. He is in the Pro Football Hall of Fame and holds the NFL record for interceptions at 81 (53 with the Vikings), a record that likely will never be broken. He played in Minnesota from 1968 to 1979 and appeared in every single game during that time.

Safety: Joey Browner

They do not come any tougher than Joey Browner. Not only did Joey excel as a defensive back, but he also contributed on special teams. He was one of the hardest hitters the team has ever had, and he was an expert at picking off passes.

Punter: Greg Coleman

Greg spent ten seasons with Minnesota and still ranks as the all-time franchise leader in punts and punt yardage. He was and still is a real tribute to the Vikings organization.

10 GREATEST MINNESOTA VIKINGS QUARTERBACKS

You think this is easy? Well, the first few are, at least for me, but it gets tougher as we go down the list.

1. Fran Tarkenton

Tarkenton's accomplishments are discussed in "All-Time Vikings Offensive Lineup," and his place among the NFL's all-time greats is tough to deny. He gave us more thrills than one could ever imagine. Fran played here for 13 seasons in two stops and led the Vikings to three Super Bowls.

2. Tommy Kramer

Tommy had some outstanding seasons for Minnesota following Tarkenton. I will never forget his last-second pass to Ahmad Rashad against Cleveland in 1980 to vault the Purple into the playoffs. He wore a Vikings uniform for 13 seasons and is second to Tarkenton on the all-time franchise list in nearly every key passing category.

3. Brad Johnson

Brad was a big, strong quarterback who had several good years here in the late 1990s and in a second stint in 2005–06. His promising career took a tough blow when he got injured in 1998. Brad was one of the real good guys and a special person to me. I got to know him well and enjoyed the success he had here and after he left the Vikings.

4. Randall Cunningham

Randall's time in Minnesota was brief—he appeared in 27 games over three seasons—but his performance in 1998 alone earns him a spot high on this list. After Brad Johnson got hurt in the second game of the 1998 season, Randall took charge at QB and went on to have one of the most productive seasons ever in the NFL. He came a missed field goal shy of leading the Vikes all the way to the Super Bowl. The 556 points scored by the Cunningham-led offense that year set a league record (since broken).

5. Daunte Culpepper

Another quarterback whose career was sidetracked by injury. Daunte's years as the Vikings' QB were among the most productive in team history. In his first season at quarterback, 2000, he topped the league with 33 TD passes while leading Minnesota to the NFC Championship Game. In 2004, he established single-season franchise records for pass completions, completion percentage, passing yards, and passing touchdowns. Daunte was never the same after his injury, suffered in 2005, and he was traded the following year. His contentious relationship with new coach Brad Childress and team management also had a lot to do with his leaving.

6. Warren Moon

During his "cup of coffee" with the Vikings from 1994 to 1996, Hall of Famer Warren Moon produced some exciting seasons and put up big numbers. He is the only Vikings quarterback ever to have two 4,000-yard passing seasons, accomplished back-to-back in '94 and '95, and he completed more than 60 percent of his passes during his Minnesota career.

7. Wade Wilson

Although he was stuck behind Tommy Kramer throughout his first several years with the Vikings, and later behind Rich Gannon in his final years, Wade emerged as a consistent starter for several seasons in Minnesota. He could really throw the football downfield and made the Pro Bowl in 1988.

(Continued)

8. Joe Kapp

Joe played eight years in the Canadian Football League before coming to Minnesota in 1967, taking over at quarterback with Tarkenton's departure to the Giants. Kapp played here for only three seasons, but his performance in 1969 as he guided the Vikings to their first Super Bowl was a classic. He left after that season due to a contract dispute and played only one more year of pro ball (for the Patriots in 1970). Kapp is a member of both the Canadian Football Hall of Fame and the College Football Hall of Fame.

9. Brett Favre

It hurts to put a longtime Green Bay Packer on my list, but Brett had a storybook season during his first year in Minnesota, throwing for more than 4,200 yards and 33 touchdowns while leading the team to a 12–4 record. His second and final year was not so good, but in that first campaign he came just one errant pass against the Saints away from taking the Purple to the promised land.

10. Rich Gannon

Gannon's career really peaked after he went to the Raiders in 1999, but he had a few good years with the Vikings earlier in the decade, serving as the primary starter from 1990 to 1992. He shared signal-calling duties with others some of the time, but I always thought he deserved more of a chance to play. He proved that he was capable later in his career.

10 GREATEST MINNESOTA VIKINGS RUNNING BACKS

We have been very fortunate to have some tremendous running backs with the Vikings. It is a pleasure to list my top ten all-time ball carriers. The first few I found easy to list. The last group is tougher, and I had to leave off some very good running backs, such as Tommy Mason, Terry Allen, and Clinton Jones.

1. Adrian Peterson
Number one, no question about it. He may go down in NFL history as the greatest running back of all time if he stays healthy. (Peterson is discussed earlier under "All-Time Vikings Offensive Lineup.")

2. Chuck Foreman
Chuck could do it all. He was an unbelievable runner and could catch passes out of the backfield. He was so dynamic with his twisting and turning running style . . . just a tremendous player. A first-round pick of the Vikings in 1973, Foreman made the Pro Bowl in each of his first five seasons in the league, and he had three straight 1,000-yard rushing seasons from 1975 to 1977.

3. Robert Smith
Robert was as graceful a running back as there ever was in football. It was a big surprise when he retired so early in his career, at the age of 28, after having perhaps the best season of his career in 2000, when he posted personal bests in rushing yards, attempts, and touchdowns. He ranks second to Peterson among Vikings running backs in lifetime rushing yardage.

(Continued)

4. Bill "Boom Boom" Brown

It's hard to think of a tougher all-around player for the Vikings than "Boom Boom." He was a bruising blocker, a terrific runner, and an excellent pass receiver out of the backfield. He was pure and true Viking all the way. Only Adrian Peterson has more carries and more rushing touchdowns than Brown in Vikings history.

5. Dave Osborn

Dave Osborn came from Cando, North Dakota, and set the bar high with his determination and never-ending passion for the game. He was a great blocker for Bill Brown and, like Brown, was an excellent runner and pass receiver in his own right. No one trained more or worked harder to improve his skills than Osborn. He played 11 seasons in Minnesota, including two Super Bowl years.

6. Darrin Nelson

Darrin had all the skills of a great running back: superb quickness and speed, good hands, and tough blocking. In addition to being Minnesota's top running option for much of the mid- to late 1980s, he also was regularly among the team's top pass catchers, and he returned kickoffs and punts for several seasons.

7. Ted Brown

Ted was an outstanding running back with the Vikings for eight seasons (1979–86). He could run with power and skill and was really tough to bring down. He was a 1,000-yard rusher in 1981 and also led the team in receptions that year with 83 catches.

8. Rickey Young

Rickey Young could run with the football and was an outstanding pass receiver as well. He was extremely versatile and used in many different ways for the Vikings from 1978 to 1983.

9. Alfred Anderson

Alfred was a tough, bruising type of running back who played with the Vikings from 1984 to 1991. A fixture in the backfield, he could be counted on to deliver the big play when needed, whether running or catching the ball.

10. Oscar Reed

"Give the seed to Oscar Reed," the fans would say. The 6-foot Reed was powerfully built and could deliver a bruising running style. He ran with reckless abandon and was really fun to watch carry the football during his seven seasons in Minnesota (1968–74).

5 GREATEST MINNESOTA VIKINGS WIDE RECEIVERS

The Minnesota Vikings have been truly blessed with some great wide receivers, several of whom played here for many years. We have been greatly entertained through the years by watching these all-time greats.

1. Cris Carter
Cris played here from 1990 to 2001 and is now a Pro Football Hall of Famer. During his tenure with the Vikings, Cris was on the receiving end of 1,004 passes for 12,383 yards and 110 touchdowns—all franchise records. He was an eight-time Pro Bowler and two-time All-Pro in his 12 Vikings seasons. Enough said.

2. Randy Moss
Randy may be the best or at least the most exciting and talented receiver who ever played the game. It is a shame that his off-field antics and occasional on-field ones often overshadowed his brilliant career. While with the Vikings from 1998 to 2004 and again, briefly, in 2010, he caught 587 passes for 9,316 yards and 92 touchdowns.

3. Anthony Carter
Anthony played here from 1985 to 1993 and had the ability to take over a football game with his outstanding skills. In his years with the Vikings, he caught 478 passes for 7,365 yards and 52 touchdowns. In a 1987 playoff game against the San Francisco 49ers, he caught ten passes for 227 yards to help the Vikings advance to the NFC Championship Game.

4. Ahmad Rashad

And to think, this great receiver was almost released by the Vikings after he was obtained from Seattle but before he even played a down for Minnesota. It took an intervention by Fran Tarkenton to GM Mike Lynn to keep Rashad in uniform. It was a good call, because he caught 400 passes for the Vikings for 5,489 yards and 34 touchdowns. His most famous TD catch was a last-minute game-winner from quarterback Tommy Kramer against the Cleveland Browns to vault the Vikings into the 1980 playoffs. Ahmad played here from 1976 to 1982 and was a four-time Pro Bowler.

5. Sammy White

Sammy played his entire NFL career here, from 1976 to 1985, and caught 393 passes for 6,400 yards and 50 touchdowns. He was a big-play receiver and caught many big-time passes in big games. His career yards-per-reception average of 16.3 is higher than any other Vikings receiver.

5 MOST MEMORABLE RANDY MOSS MOMENTS

Randy was always a story. He could be the best interview and the worst interview, depending on the day and his mood at the time. He was a sportswriter's dream, as he always seemed to give us something to write and talk about with his incredible personality and antics. Here are a few of his most *interesting* moments.

1. The Squirt Bottle Incident
During the 1999 playoffs, just his second year in the league, Randy squirted a game official with a water bottle late in a loss to the Rams. He was fined $25,000 by the league.

2. The Traffic Cop Incident
Randy was accused in 2002 of almost running over a traffic officer in Minneapolis with his vehicle. He allegedly was trying to push the officer out of the way as he was attempting to make an illegal turn. Moss was charged with assault and, after pleading guilty, was fined and ordered to perform community service.

3. The Mooning Incident
After scoring a touchdown during a nationally televised playoff game at Lambeau Field in Green Bay in 2005, Randy pretended to "moon" the crowd in the end zone. He was fined $10,000 by the league.

4. "I Play When I Want to Play"
Randy was infamous for many of his statements to the media, perhaps none more notable than his 2001 comment, "I play when I want to play," in response to criticism that he didn't always give 100-percent effort. The response didn't do much to defer that criticism.

5. The Lunch Room Incident
In 2010, after Moss returned to play for the Vikings, he loudly complained about the quality of the food being served in the lunch room at Winter Park, shouting, "Who ordered this crap? I wouldn't feed this to my dog!"

5 GREATEST MINNESOTA VIKINGS KICKERS

We have seen many a game won and lost due to the foot of a Vikings kicker. In looking back over the years, I have ranked those I believe are the five best of all time, not necessarily based on point totals only. Note that the current Vikings kicker, Blair Walsh, while in only his second year with Minnesota in 2013, may turn out to be number one on this list if he remains with the team for a lengthy period. He already has broken some team and NFL records and has proven to be a very long and accurate kicker thus far in his career.

1. **Fred Cox**
Fred played with the Vikings from 1963 to 1977 and is the all-time leading scorer in Vikings history with 1,365 points. Former Hall of Fame quarterback Fran Tarkenton once said, "If I needed an extra point or a field goal to win a game, I would want Fred Cox kicking it for us."

2. **Gary Anderson**
Although he will always be remembered for the infamous missed kick in the 1998 playoff game against the Falcons, Anderson was an incredibly accurate kicker—and that was the only kick he missed in the entire 1998 season and postseason. He scored 542 points while with the Vikings from 1998 to 2002 and had an outstanding 23-year career in the NFL.

3. **Ryan Longwell**
Ryan kicked for the Vikings from 2006 to 2010. Even though he played for Green Bay previously, he was accepted well in Minnesota and made some big kicks while here. He had a very strong leg and was also quite accurate. Longwell scored 529 points while with the Vikings.

(Continued)

4. Fuad Reveiz

The Vikings kicker from 1990 to 1995, Fuad scored 598 points for Minnesota, third on the franchise's all-time list. He made a league-high 34 field goals during his Pro Bowl season of 1994.

5. Rick Danmeier

Rick followed Fred Cox as the Vikings' kicker and was here from 1977 to 1983. He proved to be a very accurate kicker for Minnesota and scored 364 points.

5 GREATEST MINNESOTA VIKINGS PUNTERS

A lot of punters have come through Minnesota to play for the Vikings, some of whom stayed around for just a short time and others who were on the roster for many years. Here are my top five best of all time.

1. Greg Coleman

Greg was here for ten years from 1978 to 1987, a long time for a punter in the NFL. He may not have had the best overall average, but Greg was a very consistent punter for the many years he was here.

2. Chris Kluwe

Chris had the best punting average of any Vikings punter in history at 44.2 yards. He played here from 2005 to 2012 and had a longest kick of 70 yards.

3. Mitch Berger

Mitch punted (and also kicked off) for the Vikings from 1996 to 2001. He currently ranks third on the franchise list in average yards per kick at 43.5 yards, with a long of 75 yards.

4. Harry Newsome

Harry played for the Vikings as the punter for four years, 1990–93, and he ranks second in team history in punting average with 43.8 yards per kick.

5. Bobby Walden

Bobby was around in the early days under head coach Norm Van Brocklin. He averaged over 40 yards per kick in his time here, from 1964 to 1967.

5 GREAT VIKINGS WHO ALSO PLAYED FOR THE GREEN BAY PACKERS

It's hard to talk about because of the great rivalry between the Packers and the Vikings and even harder to think about a Packer wearing Vikings colors or the reverse, but here are the top five who did.

1. Brett Favre
This was the hardest to figure out. To see Brett Favre, the all-time Packers great, come out of the Minnesota Vikings locker room in 2009 wearing Vikings gear was hard to believe. It was a moment I will never forget.

2. Ryan Longwell
It seemed like Longwell made a lot of kicks for Green Bay that sunk the Vikings while he wore the green and gold from 1997 to 2005, so it was nice to have him kicking on our side, which he did from 2006 to 2011.

3. Greg Jennings
The longtime outstanding receiver for the Packers put on the purple colors beginning in the 2013 season. He made a lot of big plays over the years for Green Bay and was a two-time Pro Bowler. Hopefully, he can match those accomplishments here for the Vikings

4. Dave Osborn
Dave was a cornerstone in the backfield for the Vikings for 11 seasons before he finished out his NFL career playing one season with Green Bay. It was really tough to see Dave wearing the Packers' colors.

5. Darren Sharper
After eight years in Green Bay, Sharper jumped over to Minnesota, where he played well from 2005 to 2008, earning two Pro Bowl selections in those four seasons.

5 FIVE GREATEST MINNESOTA VIKINGS HEAD COACHES

1. Bud Grant

Obviously, an easy one here. The coach from 1967 to 1983 and again in 1985, Bud was and still is the face of the franchise. His 11 division titles and four trips to the Super Bowl cemented his Pro Football Hall of Fame career as the Vikings' coach.

2. Dennis Green

Green won four divisional titles and 97 games as head coach of the Vikings from 1992 to 2001 and led them to the memorable 15–1 season in 1998.

3. Jerry Burns

Bud Grant's longtime assistant took over as head coach of the Vikings in 1986 when Bud retired for the second time. Jerry won 52 games and led them to the playoffs three times in his short six years at the helm.

4. Norm Van Brocklin

Norm was named the Vikings' first coach in 1961 and remained with the team through the 1966 season. Although he won only 29 games in his six years with the club, leading the team to victory over the Chicago Bears in the franchise's first game was one of the greatest upset victories in NFL history.

5. Brad Childress

Childress was not here long enough to establish much of a winning record. However, other than his last season, he improved on the number of victories with each year. His best season was 2009, when Brett Favre led the Vikings to the NFC Championship Game. It was likely only an errant pass by Favre that kept the Vikings out of a fifth Super Bowl.

MY MOST MEMORABLE BUD GRANT MOMENTS

1. **Hall of Fame Induction**
Being with Bud in Canton, Ohio, as he was inducted into the Pro
Football Hall of Fame in 1994 was a special moment in my life and
broadcasting career. Bud was as emotional as I have ever seen him,
which revealed a side of him that had rarely been seen before.

2. **Jim Marshall's Retirement**
I was at Jim's private luncheon and his public retirement ceremony
at the Metrodome. Again, Bud was very emotional. I don't think
there is any question that Jim was his favorite Viking, and he
showed it when trying to talk about what Jim meant to the
Minnesota Vikings.

3. **Four Super Bowls**
Although the Vikings lost them all, it was Bud who took them to
the Super Bowl four times from 1969 to 1976, each time putting
together a remarkable run. He was the coach and the leader of
some of the greatest teams in Minnesota Vikings history.

4. **First Retirement from the Vikings**
When Bud announced he was leaving the Vikings on January 29,
1984, when he was just 56 years old, it shocked everyone. It was
hard to imagine the Vikings without Bud Grant. It was like the
universe was out of alignment. Bud Grant, not on the sidelines for
the Purple—not going to happen, never. Well, it did.

5. **All Those Central Division Titles**
Eleven of them, to be exact, all from 1968 to 1980.

6. **The 50 Greatest Vikings Reunion**
To see Bud that evening at the Minneapolis Convention Center,
with all his players from the past, was such a special moment. He
was like a proud papa. It was such an incredible gathering, and

they were all there: Tarkenton, Tingelhoff, Bill Brown, Osborn, Voigt, Marshall, Eller, Page, and the rest. What a night!

7. Bud in Short Sleeves at TCF Bank Stadium

Following the event at the Convention Center, the franchise's 50 greatest players gathered together on the field before a game was played on a snowy evening at TCF Bank Stadium. (Remember that the Dome had collapsed earlier that season.) And there was Bud Grant, wearing a short-sleeve golf shirt on that cold December day. How quickly the memories came back to those miserably cold days at old Metropolitan Stadium, with the Purple in short sleeves and without sideline heaters.

8. Interviewing Bud on *Rosen Sports Sunday* After He Announced His Retirement

Bud announced his (first) retirement in Hawaii, where Vikings President Max Winter stayed during the winter. I recall my interview with Bud after the surprise announcement. Later, it was an even greater experience to have Bud and Les Steckel, the new head coach, and several of the Vikings on my *Rosen Sports Sunday* program back in the Twin Cities.

9. Football Game in England

In August 1983, the Vikings played an exhibition game against the St. Louis Cardinals at Wembley Stadium in London. I recall Bud exiting the bus as the team arrived at the stadium and commenting, "Whose idea was this?"

10. 1969 Playoff Game against the Rams

It seemed like the signature game for Bud and the Vikings, when the team came back in the second half of the playoff matchup against the Los Angeles Rams. It was a terrific game for the Purple and led the way to the team's glory years.

5 MOST MEMORABLE DENNIS GREEN MOMENTS

When Denny Green coached the Vikings from 1992 to 2001, he proved that he was a good football coach and won a lot of games. However, his coaching tenure was also filled with some interesting times, and even a few after he left. Here are some of the most notable.

1. **Taking the Knee**
His decision to "take a knee" and let the clock run out before the end of regulation time (with two timeouts remaining) in the 1998 NFC title game against Atlanta will go down in Vikings infamy forever. The Vikings were the highest-scoring team in NFL history, and the decision did not meet with fans' approval. Minnesota went on to lose the game in overtime.

2. *No Room for Crybabies*
Green's book, entitled *No Room for Crybabies*, created incredible controversy in the organization when it was published in 1997. In the book, Green threatened to sue the team over its pursuit of Lou Holtz as a possible new head coach.

3. **Post-Game Interviews**
His media commentary often created problems, as he would fail to answer pointed questions about a game that had just been played. A typical answer such as "That is ancient history" never sat well with the media.

4. **"The High Road"**
When Green left the Vikings, he made the famous statement, "If you're looking for Denny Green, look on the high road, 'cause that is where you will find me."

5. **"They Are Who We Thought They Were"**
He wasn't with the Vikings anymore, but Green's rant in 2006, when he was head coach of the Arizona Cardinals, was classic Denny. After a loss to the Bears, Green had his infamous television press conference meltdown, when he shouted several times, "They [the Bears] are who we thought they were, and we let them off the hook!"

MY FAVORITE MINNESOTA GOPHERS FOOTBALL MEMORIES

1. 1960 Iowa Game

In one of the greatest victories in Minnesota football history, the Gophers upset the number-one ranked Iowa Hawkeyes 27–10. Led by All-Americans Sandy Stephens, Tom Brown, and Bobby Bell, the Gophers put on a dominant display at Memorial Stadium. It was a great victory for Murray Warmath and his Maroon and Gold squad, and it ultimately landed Minnesota in the Rose Bowl.

2. Walking up the Tunnel to Our Seats

Every time I walked up the tunnel at Memorial Stadium into our section and got the first glimpse of the field, it was a thrill like no other. This was Golden Gophers football, and as a kid, there was nothing better. The old Memorial Stadium was a great football atmosphere on Saturdays in the fall.

3. The Marching Band

When I was a kid at the old stadium, the band really set the tone for those Saturday fall games. The "Minnesota Rouser," "Minnesota March," "Hail! Minnesota"—the band played them all, and each one produced a chill up my back.

4. The Walk Down University Avenue

Before you even got to the game at the old Memorial Stadium— before the walk up to your seat and hearing the band—there was the walk down University Avenue with my dad. I loved every minute of it. We have that experience again with TCF Bank Stadium, and that special feeling is slowly returning to campus.

5. Minnesota, Hail to Thee

The University of Minnesota marching band playing "Hail! Minnesota" at halftime has always been a special moment for me at Gophers football games.

(Continued)

6. Public Address Announcer Jules Perlt

There will never be another like him. His voice, the resonance, and his unique emphasis on certain things helped him stand apart from all others. "Annnnnnderson makes it a first down on the tennnn!" "Bellllllll stopping that play!" There will never be anyone better than Jules Perlt. How about the inverted score announcement. "Final score: Iowa 6, Illinois 12!"

7. Barber and Maroney

The mid-2000s was a tremendous time in Gophers football history, as we were able to watch the great running backs Marion Barber and Laurence Maroney play together under head coach Glen Mason. They formed one of the best running back duos in college football history.

8. Gophers Beat Michigan 16–0, October 22, 1967

This has to go down as one of the greatest Gophers victories and also one of the biggest upsets in college football history. Michigan came into Minneapolis as a heavy favorite and got the stuffing knocked out of them by a fired-up Gophers squad. It was a great day that I will always remember.

9. Bobby Bell, Carl Eller, and Sandy Stephens

The Gophers have had many great football players through the years, but few were greater than Bobby Bell, Sandy Stephens, and Carl Eller in the early 1960s. Each played a dominating role to lead the Maroon and Gold to many memorable victories, including back-to-back Rose Bowls.

10. O. J. Simpson

I know, I know, he's in prison now and has had a terrible and tragic history since leaving football. But make no mistake: he was one of the greatest college and professional football players to ever play the game. I recall when the USC Trojans came to Minneapolis with O. J. to play the Gophers. It was a thrill to see him in action.

10 GREATEST MINNESOTA GOPHERS FOOTBALL PLAYERS

1. Bronko Nagurski

When you're an All-American at two positions, you must be a pretty good football player. Bronko was just that, maybe the best ever.

2. Bruce Smith

Bruce is the only Gophers football player to win the Heisman Trophy. He was an outstanding running back for Minnesota in the 1940s.

3. Bobby Bell

Bobby starred on offense and defense for the Gophers in the early 1960s, and he went on to a Hall of Fame career in the pros playing for the Kansas City Chiefs. He was a two-time All-American with the Gophers and won the Outland Trophy as college football's top lineman in 1962.

4. Carl Eller

Carl was an unstoppable defensive end and tackle for the Gophers and one of the greatest to ever wear the maroon and gold. He was a tremendous pass rusher, and he carried his traits into the NFL.

5. Sandy Stephens

Sandy led the Gophers to the Rose Bowl in 1961 and 1962 as an outstanding quarterback and defensive back. He was an unstoppable option-type quarterback and the leader of the 1960 national championship team. Sandy was also the first African-American quarterback at a major university to earn All-American status.

(Continued)

6. Tom Brown

Tom was an unbelievable player at guard on offense and defense for the Gophers. He won the Outland Trophy in 1960 before going on to a Hall of Fame career as a pro in Canada.

7. Paul Giel

A two-time All-American, Paul was a terrific running back in the early 1950s and was named the Big Ten Most Valuable Player in 1952 and 1953. Paul could have had a career in the NFL but instead went to play Major League Baseball. He later became the longtime athletic director at the university, and before that he worked on Vikings radio broadcasts.

8. Bud Grant

Bud earned nine letters as a Gopher, four in football and the others in baseball and basketball. He was perhaps the best all-around athlete to ever enroll at Minnesota. His coaching legacy got him into the Pro Football Hall of Fame and the Canadian Football Hall of Fame.

9. Leo Nomellini

Leo was a dominant lineman for the Gophers in the 1940s, twice earning All-American recognition. He was an outstanding player on both sides of the ball and went on to a Hall of Fame career with the San Francisco 49ers in the NFL.

10. Francis "Pug" Lund

Pug Lund was a great halfback for Minnesota in the 1930s and was a terrific ball carrier. His name is legendary in Gophers history. In 1934, he was named MVP of the Big Ten and selected as an All-American.

5 GREATEST MINNESOTA GOPHERS FOOTBALL COACHES

Since the beginning of Minnesota Golden Gophers football going back to 1883, a total of 31 different men have served as head coach of the Gophers. In some years, more than one person was on record as the head coach. Here are my top five of all time, mostly with respect to their overall record while coaching at Minnesota.

1. Bernie Bierman

It isn't even close. Bernie won five national championships during his years with the Gophers, from 1932 to 1941 and then again from 1945 to 1950. He won 93 games as head coach.

2. Henry Williams

Williams won 136 games and lost only 33 in 22 seasons as head coach from 1900 to 1921. The Gophers won eight Big Ten championships under Williams. Williams Arena on the University of Minnesota campus is named after him.

3. Murray Warmath

Murray won 87 games during his tenure from 1954 to 1971 and took the Golden Gophers to back-to-back Rose Bowls following the 1960 and 1961 seasons. His 1960 team won the national championship.

4. Glen Mason

Mason coached here from 1997 to 2006 and won 64 games. He was known for his development of a strong game, and he coached some of the best running backs in Gophers history.

5. Cal Stoll

Following Murray Warmath's 18 years at the helm, Stoll coached here for seven seasons (1972–78) and won 39 games. He was a popular coach among players and fans even though he finished with a .500 winning percentage.

10 BEST THINGS ABOUT TCF BANK STADIUM

1. AND 2. On-Campus and Outdoor Football

We waited a long time, and finally we have football back on campus at the University of Minnesota. And it was worth the wait because TCF Bank Stadium is a spectacular place to watch a football game—outdoors! It is a great stadium, no doubt about that, but the best part is being outdoors again and right on the university campus where it belongs!

3. The View

The stadium offers a tremendous view from the open west end toward Minneapolis. It allows us to see the campus and the city— just beautiful!

4. The Colors

There is maroon and gold everywhere, and all the other colors really accentuate the stadium, much like at Target Field. The green stadium turf, the stands, the seats, the outside and inside structure, the scoreboard, the inner corridors—all phenomenal.

5. The Pageantry

The stadium brings out everything that you would want as a fan for an on-campus football stadium. With the marching band and all that goes with the stadium, great Saturdays in the fall have returned!

6. University Avenue

One of my fondest memories as a kid was walking down University Avenue to Memorial Stadium. This was all lost with the Metrodome, and now we have that experience once again. The walk down University Avenue and the ambiance that goes with it has returned to campus.

7. Night Football

The Saturday afternoon games are occasionally replaced with night football, and I have to say it is a spectacular experience. All that I have said about the stadium is in many ways accentuated even more under the bright lights of Big Ten football at night.

8. The Press Box

TCF has a spectacular press box for the media, allowing us to enjoy the game and get our work done. Great space, great seats, great view—just a special place!

9. AND 10. Comfortable Seats Close to the Field

For the fans, the seats are spacious and close to the field. I have heard many times that there is not a bad seat at TCF Bank Stadium. From every place in the stadium, the view is excellent, and you never have the feeling of being light-years away from the action.

BASEBALL

MY FAVORITE TWINS MOMENTS

1. **Winning 1987 and 1991 World Series**
This has to be number one of all time. Every year, all the major league teams go to spring training with one thing in mind, to win the World Series. And the Twins did it twice in five years. Thrilling times for Twins fans!

2. **Airplane Ride Back from Detroit after Clinching 1987 ALCS**
After the Twins defeated the Detroit Tigers to advance to the 1987 World Series, the ride back from Detroit on the plane was so special and exciting, and it's at the top of my list of favorite Twins moments. I felt like I was with a bunch of Little Leaguers who had just won a big game. The guys were all just terrific, and they included me in on all the fun.

3. **Entering the Metrodome for the Fan Celebration**
When we arrived back in the Twin Cities after winning the Detroit series in 1987 and entered the Metrodome for a celebration, nobody could have believed what was in store for the Twins and the reception they got. The place was packed, and the cheering was spectacular. It was very emotional, and I don't think there is anybody from the team or in the entourage who will ever forget that evening.

4. **Game 6 of the 1991 World Series**
Kirby did it all in this game. First, he made an unbelievable catch in center field to rob the Braves of a potential run-scoring hit, and then he hit the game-winning home run in extra innings. He truly carried the Twins on his back, as he said he would. I will never forget his performance in that game.

(Continued)

5. Kent Hrbek's Grand Slam in 1987 World Series

There were a lot of thrills in the 1987 World Series, but none was greater than Kent Hrbek's grand slam in the sixth game. The blast over the center field fence at the Metrodome helped to put the Twins one win away from capturing their first World Series championship.

6. Game 7 of the 1991 World Series

Perhaps other than New York Yankees pitcher Don Larsen throwing a perfect game in the 1956 World Series, Jack Morris' performance in the seventh game of the 1991 series may be the greatest World Series game ever pitched. His ten shutout innings led the Twins to their second title in a span of five seasons.

7. Rod Carew in the Summer of 1977

What a great season that was for Rod Carew! It had been 36 years since any major-leaguer batted .400 in a season; Ted Williams of the Boston Red Sox hit .406 in 1941. Rod flirted with .400 for most of the season and was at .401 as late as July 10, but he eventually dropped to .388 on the year—still good enough for the highest single-season average in 20 years and one of Rod's seven career batting crowns.

8. Harmon Killebrew's 500th Home Run

I covered this game for WCCO television. Harmon actually hit two homers that night, and I interviewed him after the game. I actually felt kind of bad for him, because there was little media attention given to his accomplishment, especially compared to what we see today with such milestones. And Harmon, in his usual humbleness, talked more about the Twins losing the game than he did his 500th home run.

9. Game 2 of the 1965 World Series

Sandy Koufax had always been my favorite pitcher, but it was quite the thrill to see the Twins defeat the mighty Sandy in Game 2 of the 1965 World Series, a game and a day that will be in my memory bank forever. Just one day after beating another future Hall of Famer in Don Drysdale, the Twins managed to score two runs off Koufax and knocked him out of the game before winning 5–1.

10. Bob Allison's Catch in the 1965 Series

We are still at the 1965 World Series, and I'm talking about the great running, sliding catch made by Twins left fielder Bob Allison down the left field foul line on a hit by Dodger Jim Lefebvre. I can still see Bob coming up with the ball. It seemed impossible that he would get there in time, but he made the play!

MINNESOTA TWINS ALL-TIME LINEUP

To be honest, this was a fairly easy list for me to come up with. We have had some great star players here, and it was fun thinking about them all being in the same lineup. Putting together my all-time batting order was a lot tougher.

Catcher: Joe Mauer
There is no question about Joe being the catcher. He has been an outstanding player behind the plate and an incredible pure hitter. In just his first ten years in the league, Joe has earned three batting titles, three Gold Glove Awards, six All-Star selections, and an American League MVP Award. His batting average as a catcher ranks among the all-time best.

First Base: Kent Hrbek
This was a tough call between Herbie and Justin Morneau, so I'll insert Justin as my designated hitter. Kent was a mainstay at first base for 14 seasons and an all-time fan favorite. He was an outstanding hitter and an excellent fielder on two World Series champions. His 293 career homers rank behind only Killebrew on the franchise list.

Second Base: Rod Carew
No question here. Rod was one of the greatest hitters of all time and an excellent fielder—a Hall of Famer. He led the American League in batting seven times with the Twins, and his flirtation with .400 in 1977 was a magical season. He was the Rookie of the Year in 1967, the AL MVP in 1977, and an All-Star in every one of his 12 seasons in Minnesota.

Shortstop: Zoilo Versalles
Zoilo was a tremendous player in the early years for the Twins. The Cuban-born infielder could field, hit, run, and hit for power on occasion. He won the American League MVP Award during the pennant season of 1965.

Third Base: Harmon Killebrew
There just is not enough space to list all of Harmon's accomplishments, attributes, and abilities. He was one of the greatest home run hitters of all time and the greatest Twin of all. He led the league in homers five times in Minnesota (and once more with the Washington Senators) and was named the 1969 AL MVP thanks to his league-best 49 home runs and 140 RBI. Nobody has played more games in a Twins uniform than "Killer," and nobody has hit more homers or driven in more runs for the organization.

Left Field: Bob Allison
Bob was a solid home run hitter and excellent fielder for the Twins from the inaugural season in Minnesota through 1970. He was one of the leaders on the club during the Twins' first World Series, against the Dodgers in 1965, and he made one of the greatest catches ever in the World Series that year.

Center Field: Kirby Puckett
Kirby was probably the most popular player in Twins history. He could do it all: run, throw, field, and hit. The franchise's all-time hits leader, Kirby was an All-Star in ten of his 12 seasons and won six Gold Glove Awards. His heroics in the 1991 World Series—the leaping catch and game-winning home run in Game 6—were the stuff of legend. He was simply a terrific ballplayer with an infectious personality and a bona fide baseball Hall of Famer.

Right Field: Tony Oliva
Tony O could really hit the baseball. To some baseball experts and historians, he ranks among the best pure hitters of all time, and many wonder why he is not enshrined in Cooperstown. Tony led the American League in hits five times and in batting average three times—including during his rookie year of 1964—and was named to the All-Star team in each of his first eight seasons in the majors.

Designated Hitter: Justin Morneau

I'm glad the American League has the DH, because there needs to be a spot for Justin in this lineup. After all, he is an American League MVP (2006) and one of the franchise's top home run hitters and run producers. Justin was also an outstanding fielder. Who knows what he might have accomplished if concussion issues hadn't set him back.

Right-Handed Starting Pitcher: Bert Blyleven

Bert came up to the Twins in 1970 as a 19-year-old kid and fascinated us with his curveball, one of the best ever. Bert is a Hall of Famer and my choice as the all-time best Twins pitcher, although we have had some good ones! He won 149 games in two stays with the Twins, 11 years in all, and is the franchise leader in strikeouts and complete games. Bert is also one of the greatest characters in baseball history.

Left-Handed Starting Pitcher: Frank Viola

Frankie V. was a member of the Twins' great rookie class of 1982, and within a couple of years he established himself as one of the top lefties in all of baseball. He won a lot of games for mediocre Twins teams in the mid-1980s before helping to catapult them to the World Series in 1987. He earned the World Series MVP Award with victories in Games 1 and 7. "Sweet Music" was even better the next year, winning the AL Cy Young Award with a league-best 24 wins.

Relief Pitcher: Joe Nathan

The all-time franchise leader in career saves (260), Nathan was a lights-out closer for seven seasons in Minnesota. He averaged more than 40 saves per season from 2004 to 2009 and was named to the AL All-Star team four times.

MINNESOTA TWINS ALL-TIME BATTING ORDER

The only thing I have to say about this lineup and batting order is that I sure would like to be the manager delivering it to the home plate umpire. And since this is the American League, we'll make use of the designated hitter, rather than making Bert wield a bat.

1. Rod Carew, 2B
A great hitter to all fields, and also a terrific base runner. He could hit first or second.

2. Joe Mauer, C
Joe will go down in baseball history as the greatest catcher and one of the best hitters ever. Fits well in the two slot.

3. Tony Oliva, RF
Tony is a great number-three hitter. Maybe the best hitter in the lineup, and he could hit with power.

4. Harmon Killebrew, 3B
Who else would bat clean-up but this all-time home run giant?

5. Kent Hrbek, 1B
Herbie and Kirby could be reversed in the order. Kent was a good hitter and could hit with power.

6. Kirby Puckett, CF
Again, a good hitter with good power.

7. Justin Morneau, DH
He could hit for both average and power.

8. Bob Allison, LF
A guy with more than 250 career home runs batting eighth!?! I'd hate to be on the mound facing this lineup.

9. Zoilo Versalles, SS
Zoilo was a good leadoff man for the Twins in his day, but here he serves as a "second leadoff hitter" at the end of the lineup.

10 GREATEST MINNESOTA TWINS HITTERS

1. Harmon Killebrew
Although he didn't hit for a high average (.256 over his career), Harmon's home run power was simply awe-inspiring. He is a member of the 500 home run club, and he generated many titanic shots that looked like they would never land. His monster blast into the second deck at the old Met Stadium in 1967 was unheard of at the time.

2. Tony Oliva
Tony was one of the best and purest hitters in baseball history. Only the injured knees that shortened his career have kept him out of the Baseball Hall of Fame. Maybe someday.

3. Rod Carew
Rod was a pleasure to watch—so graceful and such a great overall ballplayer. His .334 lifetime average with the Twins is the highest in franchise history.

4. Joe Mauer
How many more batting titles will Joe win before he is done? He is one of the toughest outs in baseball.

5. Kent Hrbek
A .282 lifetime hitter, Kent batted over .300 three times and had plenty of power. He also came through in the clutch. Remember his three-run homer to beat the Yankees in New York in his first year? Or his grand slam in the 1987 World Series?

6. Kirby Puckett

Kirby batted .318 for his career, and he never hit lower than .288 in a season. He also could hit the longball (207 homers in his career) and was known to deliver big-time hits. His home run to win Game 6 of the 1991 World Series may be the biggest in franchise history.

7. Justin Morneau

In his MVP season of 2006, he finished in the top ten in the league in both average (.321) and homers (34). He hit for both average and power throughout much of his Twins career.

8. Paul Molitor

Paul ranks eighth on the list only because his time with the Twins was short. But in those three seasons in Minnesota, the Hall of Famer batted .312, and in 1996 he led the league with 225 hits, adding to the 3,000-plus for his career.

9. Jimmie Hall

Jimmie had some good home run years in his short time as the Twins' center fielder, averaging nearly 25 homers per season over four years.

10. Dave Winfield

Dave was past his prime by the time he came to Minnesota, but he was still a dangerous hitter, even in his 40s.

5 MOST MEMORABLE TWINS HOME RUNS

Minnesota Twins players have hit some memorable home runs since the inception of the franchise in 1961. I'm sure most Twins fans have their favorites because they were at the ballpark and witnessed the blast in person or happened to catch the pivotal moment on television. These are the five that I recall that will stay with me forever.

1. **Harmon Killebrew, July 11, 1965**
With the Twins trailing the New York Yankees at Metropolitan Stadium by a score of 5–4, Harmon Killebrew hit a game-winning two-run home run in the bottom of the ninth inning to send the Twins into the All-Star break with a dramatic victory. The Twins went on to win the pennant that year.

2. **Kirby Puckett, Game 6 of the 1991 World Series**
With the Twins trailing the Atlanta Braves three games to two in the series, Kirby Puckett hit a home run in the bottom of the 11th inning to win it for the Twins. It was the ultimate capper on a great game for Puckett.

3. **Kent Hrbek, Game 6 of the 1987 World Series**
In the sixth game of the 1987 World Series with the Twins trailing the St. Louis Cardinals three games to two, Kent Hrbek hit a dramatic grand slam in the bottom of the sixth inning to put the Twins up 10–5 and seal the victory to force a Game 7.

4. **Harmon Killebrew, June 3, 1967**
It happened only once in the history of baseball at Metropolitan Stadium: On this date, Harmon Killebrew came to the plate and hit a ball into the upper deck at the stadium. It has been said that visiting players coming to the Met would often stand at home plate in amazement as they looked out to the upper deck to where the ball landed.

5. Harmon Killebrew, August 10, 1971

Harmon Killebrew's historic 500th career home run at Metropolitan Stadium.

5b. Julio Becquer, July 4, 1961

Okay, I have to add one more here. In the first game of a Fourth of July doubleheader against the White Sox, backup outfielder and first baseman Julio Becquer came to the plate as a pinch hitter in the bottom of the ninth inning. With two out and the bases loaded and the Twins trailing 4–2, Becquer hit a grand slam to win it for the Twins. It was one of only 12 home runs he hit in his entire major league career.

10 GREATEST MINNESOTA TWINS PITCHERS

1. Jack Morris
The St. Paul Highland Park kid hit it big in the major leagues and brought his fame and talents back home for one memorable season in 1991. Who will ever forget his magnificent performance in Game 7 of that year's World Series, when he pitched ten shutout innings to lead the team to another title? Simply one of the greatest games ever pitched in World Series history. He won 18 games during the regular season and earned the starting job for the American League in the annual All-Star Game.

2. Bert Blyleven
Bert's career accomplishments are discussed earlier under the "All-Time Lineup," but it's undeniable that this Hall of Famer is one of the best all-time pitchers and one of the greatest personalities ever to play the game. He may have been the best curveball pitcher of all time.

3. Joe Nathan
Joe gave us so many great years. After coming to Minnesota in the A. J. Pierzynski trade in 2004, he emerged as one of the premier closers in all of Major League Baseball. He ranks first on the franchise's all-time saves list with 260.

4. Eddie Guardado
"Everyday Eddie" won the hearts and souls of the Minnesota baseball faithful with his pitching prowess and his personality. He came to the Twins as a starter in 1993 but soon moved to the bullpen, working mostly as a middle-innings and setup guy for nearly a decade before taking over the closer role. In 2002, he led the league with 45 saves. He then chipped in with 41 saves (second in the AL) the following year before departing as a free agent.

5. Frank Viola

Frankie was a top-notch left-handed starter for the Twins. More than just a great hurler, he was a class act as well. He won more than 100 games in less than eight seasons with the club and won the American League Cy Young Award in 1988 with a 24–7 record and 2.64 ERA. It was tough to see him go to the New York Mets the next year.

6. Johan Santana

Another award-winning lefty for the Twins, Santana was one of the top starting pitchers in the majors in the mid-2000s. He won the Cy Young Award in 2004 and again in 2006 while leading the league in both ERA and strikeouts those years; he also led the AL in wins in 2006. Money, once again, changed everything, and Johan departed for greener pastures in New York, as he signed with the Mets in 2008.

7. Camilo Pascual

Camilo was a star of the rotation when the Washington Senators moved to Minnesota in 1961, and he was a mainstay on the staff for six more seasons in Minnesota. Another righty with an incredible curveball, the Cuban-born Pascual was a top strikeout pitcher (he led the league three years in a row, 1961–63) and a multiyear All-Star.

(Continued)

8. Jim Kaat

Jim was an outstanding and reliable left-handed pitcher and a great all-around player. He won 12 consecutive Gold Glove Awards at the position, and he was good with the bat in the days when pitchers were required to hit. In 1966, "Kitty" won a franchise-record 25 games, and he ranks first on the all-time wins list for the Twins as well (190). Jim played major league ball for 25 seasons and then went on to an excellent career in the broadcast booth, where he has been just as successful as he was on the mound.

9. Brad Radke

In Brad's 12 seasons with the Twins, he recorded 148 wins for teams that didn't win a lot of games. In just his third major league season, he notched 20 wins for a Twins club that finished 68–94. He also was one of the most popular players during his tenure with the team.

10. Jim "Mudcat" Grant

I loved to watch "Mudcat" pitch. He was so smooth and effective, and he was also a fan favorite as a pitcher for the Twins from 1964 to 1967. Grant won a league-best 21 games for the pennant-winning Twins of 1965.

5 GREATEST PITCHING PERFORMANCES BY A MINNESOTA TWIN

In the 50-plus years the Twins have been here, we have seen some great pitching performances. There have been playoff and World Series wins, no-hitters, and many great strikeout games. Here are my top five best games ever by a Minnesota Twins pitcher.

1. **Jack Morris, Game 7 of the 1991 World Series**
Number one in my book, and in most other Twins fans' books too, has to be the seventh game of the 1991 World Series. In the winner-take-all clincher, Jack pitched ten shutout innings before the Twins finally won the game in the last of the tenth. Many call the 1991 series against the Braves one of the greatest ever played, and Jack's performance probably ranks second only to New York Yankee Don Larsen's perfect game in the 1956 World Series.

2. **Johan Santana, August 19, 2007**
In a game against the Texas Rangers at the Metrodome, Johan struck out 17 batters over eight innings to set a Twins record. He struck out two in the first inning, fanned the side in the second, and struck out two in the third and fourth while retiring the first 12 batters he faced. Johan allowed only two hits in the game and walked none. He finished his time on the mound by striking out the side in the eighth before Joe Nathan came in to secure the save in the ninth.

(Continued)

3. Frank Viola, Game 7 of the 1987 World Series

In the deciding game of the 1987 World Series, Frankie "Sweet Music" Viola was the winning pitcher to lead the Twins to their first World Series championship. After allowing two runs in the second inning, Viola retired the next ten batters he faced and took control of the game, allowing just two more St. Louis Cardinals base runners. He struck out seven batters and walked none in his eight innings before handing the ball to closer Jeff Reardon, who came in for the bottom of the ninth to seal the 4–2 victory.

4. Jim Kaat, Game 2 of the 1965 World Series

In a matchup of star hurlers, Kaat faced off against the legendary Sandy Koufax in the second game of the World Series between the Twins and the Los Angeles Dodgers on October 7, 1965. Jim pitched a complete game, while Koufax was knocked out after six innings, and the Twins won by a score of 5–1.

5. Pedro Ramos, April 11, 1961

In the opening game of the 1961 season between the Minnesota Twins and New York Yankees—the first Twins game in franchise history—Cuban-born pitcher Pedro Ramos threw a complete-game shutout against the mighty New Yorkers, giving up only three hits in the 6–0 whitewashing.

MY FAVORITE TWINS, NUMBERS 1 TO 10

When I think about a particular number, I have a habit of thinking about a player who wore that number. With the Twins, when I think of the uniform and the number on the back, here is who I immediately think about wearing that number.

1. Billy Martin
Of course, Billy was a favorite beyond wearing number 1 on his uniform. He was not only a great baseball manager and so knowledgeable about the game; he was a real character and a sports reporter's dream. There was always a story when Billy Martin was around. Billy served as a scout and a third base coach for the Twins before taking over as the manager in 1969. He led the Twins to a division title in his one year on the job. A legendary bar fight with one of his pitchers, Dave Boswell, that August contributed to his being fired after the season.

2. Zoilo Versalles
Zoilo was a tremendous player and versatile shortstop for the Twins from 1961 through 1967. Every time I see the back of a uniform with number 2 on it, I think of Zoilo.

3. Harmon Killebrew
Harmon was off the charts as a quality human being. He was maybe the best example of any professional athlete when it came to being a role model for kids. And on top of his great character was incredible skill and talent with the baseball bat. Harmon brought more thrills to Twins fans than any player in team history.

4. Bob Allison
The first thing that comes to mind when I think of Bob is his incredible sliding catch down the left field foul line during the 1965 World Series. Bob was an outstanding ballplayer for the Twins and a really good guy.

(Continued)

5. Michael Cuddyer

I was sad to see Michael leave the Twins after playing here for a decade. More than just a good ballplayer, he was a great community and clubhouse guy. He was so skilled and versatile, able to play pretty much any position—he even pitched an inning for the Twins in 2011—and he could hit for power and drive in runs.

6. Tony Oliva

I can still see the number 6 emblazoned on Tony O's back, his classic stance, and his line-drive base hits. What a player!

7. Joe Mauer

Joe will go down in history as one of the best hitters to ever play the game and certainly as one of the best all-time catchers. He'll likely be remembered by the pitchers who faced him as one of the toughest outs in the game.

8. Gary Gaetti

The G-Man! Gary came up through the Twins' farm system and was a star player on the World Series teams in 1987 and 1991. He was an outstanding third baseman, a power hitter, and a fan favorite.

9. Gene Larkin

Larkin was a .266 lifetime hitter who spent only seven seasons with the Twins, but his base hit in the bottom of the tenth inning to drive in the game- and series-winning run in the seventh game of the 1991 World Series will ensure him a place in the memories of Minnesota fans. It was a tremendous ending to a tremendous World Series, giving the Twins their second world championship in five years.

10. Earl Battey

Earl was the star catcher for the early Twins teams, from 1961 to 1967. He could hit, hit with power, and run and was an outstanding defensive catcher. He was a mainstay in the lineup and was also well liked by the fans. When I think of the number 10, I can still see Earl crouching behind the plate or standing in the batter's box.

10 MORE FAVORITE MINNESOTA TWINS NUMBERS

12. Cesar Tovar

Cesar could do it all as one of the most versatile players the Twins have ever had on their roster. He once played every position in a single game as a tribute to what he was capable of doing on the field. Beyond that novelty, Cesar was also a great base stealer and once collected more than 200 hits in a season.

14. Kent Hrbek

Kent grew up right in Bloomington, near the old Metropolitan Stadium, and ended up playing for the hometown Minnesota Twins for his entire 14-year career. He assured his place as a fan favorite when he turned down significantly more money to remain a Twin. His grand slam in the 1987 World Series still stands out as one of the great Twins moments.

15. Bill Dailey

Bill was always one of my favorite Twins. He had a very short career, but he was good out of the bullpen for the Twins in 1963. There was something about Bill that really has stayed with me through the years. I enjoyed his spirit and competiveness.

16. Frank Viola

Frankie "Sweet Music" Viola was another of my favorite players and personalities. He was a great starter for the Twins for many years and really captured the hearts of the fans.

17. Camilo Pascual

Camilo was one of our best pitchers. What an incredible curveball he had. Your heart would drop when that breaking ball seemed to fall off the cliff.

(Continued)

28. Bert Blyleven

Bert is finally in the Baseball Hall of Fame in Cooperstown, and it is unbelievable that it took so long for him to get in. He was one of the greatest curveball pitchers. Bert is now the color analyst on Twins television broadcasts, and he gives great insight into the game. He will always be one of my favorites.

29. Rod Carew

Rod was one of the best hitters ever and also an excellent second baseman. I still recall the amazing steals of home during his career and the season he toyed with hitting .400. What a year that was!

34. Kirby Puckett

"Now batting for the Twins . . . Number 34 . . . Kirrrbyyy Puckett!" The words from public address announcer Bob Casey are as immortal as Kirby was on the field. There will never be another like him. His enthusiasm and love for the game goes unmatched along with his fan popularity.

36. Jim Kaat

"Kitty" Kaat was one of the best left-handers in the game, and he was a good hitter and fielder too. He really left his mark with the Twins and has continued to do so in baseball as a broadcaster. A class act all the way.

48. Torii Hunter

It was another sad day in Minnesota Twins history when Torii Hunter left as a free agent. He roamed center field here for a long time, making amazing catches in the field and delivering big hits at the plate. It was hard to believe when he returned to Minnesota wearing another team's jersey.

TOP 10 MINNESOTA TWINS CHARACTERS

The Minnesota Twins have been around here for more than 50 seasons, and during that time we have had the good fortune to see some great characters take the field. Here are my ten favorites.

1. Kirby Puckett

Kirby was one of the best players and greatest characters. A Hall of Famer in many ways. He loved to talk and loved to have fun. He was always a terrific interview!

2. Bert Blyleven

This Hall of Famer was one of the legendary characters of the game, and he still is as a broadcaster. He just loves a good laugh. He is known as one of the game's best practical jokers.

3. Mickey Hatcher

One of the game's true characters. He had a fun-loving approach to baseball, and you were never sure what Mickey might come up with next. He was known for such things as hitting a home run and then sprinting all the way around the bases. This antic led an announcer to comment, "He's running because he thinks they may take the home run off the board."

4. Lew Ford

Lew was fun to cover and had an interesting personality—you were never quite sure what he might say next. He was widely rumored to have burned himself while ironing a shirt that he was wearing, and although it's not true, it was believable as something Lew might do.

(Continued)

5. Kent Hrbek

Kent was a great player, and he liked to have fun. During the seventh game of the 1987 World Series, he played a classic practical joke on public address announcer Bob Casey with a shaving cream-filled towel.

6. Juan Berenguer

Juan was loved by the fans and could really get the crowd going. What a great smile!

7. Billy Martin

You never knew what Billy was going to do next. He was a great entertainer and a better interview when he returned as the Yankees' manager.

8. A. J. Pierzynski

He was loved when he was here and hated when he returned in a different uniform. That's A. J., but he was an outstanding catcher and a first-rate clutch hitter.

9. Frank Quilici

Frank really knew baseball and was a great interview during his years as the Twins' manager from 1972 to 1975.

10. Gene Mauch

Gene was another manager who truly knew the game. He always had a lot to say and had the experiences to back them up, with his long career in pro ball.

5 BEST MINNESOTA TWINS MANAGERS

The Twins have been a ballclub that has not needed to regularly change managers. In fact, they have had only two managers— Tom Kelly and Ron Gardenhire—since 1987. Over the past 50-plus years, the Twins have had some good skippers. One great one who doesn't make the cut but is worthy of mention is Billy Martin, who managed for one year in Minnesota (1969) and led the team to a division title but was fired by owner Calvin Griffith after the season.

1. Tom Kelly

TK won 1,140 games as manager of the Minnesota Twins from 1986 to 2001 and won two World Series with the team. A great student of the game, he was known for respecting the game and teaching that respect to his players.

2. Ron Gardenhire

"Gardy" has been a great follower of Tom Kelly in preaching respect for the game and baseball fundamentals. Through the 2013 season, he had won 998 games with the Twins and led them to a division title six times, more than any other Twins skipper.

3. Sam Mele

Sam was the franchise's first manager when it moved from Washington in 1961, and five years later he took the Twins to the 1965 World Series against the Dodgers. Sam won 524 games as manager of the Twins from 1961 to 1967.

(Continued)

4. Gene Mauch

A purist of the game, Gene Mauch managed the Twins from 1974 to 1980. Although the team wallowed in the middle of the standings during that time, he won 378 games as the Twins' manager and led them to three winning seasons in five years.

5. Frank Quilici

Frank, who preceded Mauch from 1972 to 1975, has been a Twins ambassador for many years before and after his term as manager. He won 280 games and lost 287 as the Twins' skipper.

5 BEST THINGS ABOUT RON GARDENHIRE

Ron Gardenhire has been the Minnesota Twins' manager since 2002 and recently signed another contract to manage for two more years. He has a sound baseball mind and is tremendously loyal to the Twins organization and its fans. He is well liked by his players and coaches.

1. Knows Baseball
Ron has one of the most knowledgeable baseball minds that I've ever known. He truly understands the game and knows what it takes to win.

2. Loves and Respects the Game
It's easy to tell how much Gardy loves the game. When his players play the way the game is supposed to be played, it is obvious that he is as pleased as he could be.

3. Consistent
Gardy's behavior and attitude rarely change. Whether the Twins are winning or losing, he is consistent with his expectations. He can be openly disappointed and often angry when things are going badly and the game is not respected. This does not change regardless of the team's record.

4. Loves to Go to Work
I doubt there is much Ron Gardenhire would rather do than manage the Minnesota Twins. You can tell he puts his full heart and soul into his work and aims for success at every level. He has been a very successful manager for many years and is widely respected throughout the major leagues.

5. Puts Players in Position to Succeed
Following in the makeup of Tom Kelly, Gardy does an outstanding job of putting players in a position to succeed. He knows the players' strengths and weaknesses and utilizes this knowledge to help them become successful.

10 BEST THINGS ABOUT TARGET FIELD

Over the decades, there have been many great and historic ballparks, and many remain in use. In my opinion and that of many baseball experts, Target Field, home of the Minnesota Twins since 2010, is one of the best ballparks ever built. It is an absolute joy to attend a game here, and the fans have shown their appreciation by showing up in droves.

1. Outdoor Baseball
Target Field and the Twins cannot take all the credit for this, because the Minnesota baseball community craved for the return of outdoor baseball. I'm not saying that a vacant field with some makeshift bleachers would have been satisfying, but Target Field has it all—and being outside makes it that much more enjoyable.

2. The View of Downtown Minneapolis
The view of downtown Minneapolis from the seats, especially from the third base side, is spectacular in every respect, whether during sunny afternoon games or when the skyline lights up at night.

3. Baseball Sightlines
I have heard it said many times that there is not a bad seat in the house, no matter what section you are in. Even from the concourse, you can keep an eye on the game while waiting in line for food or simply exploring the different areas of the park.

4. The Layout
The ballpark has so much beauty going for it that the experience is enjoyable in every respect—everything from the wide corridors, the available food options, the sightlines, the artwork and sculptures, the plaza area, the skyline view, and so much more.

5. The Food

Well, I like to eat, and the food at Target Field is extraordinary. This ballpark knows how to satisfy the hungry appetite. My favorites are the classic ballpark items such as the hot dogs, pizza, and ice cream (although not quite as good as those 25-cent malt cups at the old Met). But there is so much variety to enjoy at Target Field, from Tony O's Cuban sandwiches to the famous Murray's Steak Sandwich to Minnesota State Fair classics such as Walleye on a Stick.

6. The Press Box

I have been in a lot of press boxes and have covered a lot of games in my 40-plus years with WCCO television, and I can say that many of those press boxes leave a great deal to be desired. At Target Field, the press box is spacious, with plenty of room to work, and the view of the field and the crowd is perfect. It is a great place to cover a ballgame.

7. Scoreboards

Another big *wow!* The scoreboards are beautiful and colorful and really add to the game, both with special effects and by providing tons of useful information and facts to allow for a fuller enjoyment and understanding of the game.

(Continued)

8. Right Field Wall

It may not quite compare with Fenway Park's Green Monster, but Target Field's right field wall has unique and distinguishing qualities. First, it is beautiful to look at, with a design that fits right in with the rest of the ballpark. It is kind of like the "outfield porch" that you see in some ballparks, but it is a little deeper and harder to hit over than most. The overhanging portion that juts over the field also creates some interesting challenges for right fielders!

9. Intimate Setting in Downtown

It almost feels like they took a part of downtown Minneapolis, stretched it out a bit, and then fit this beautiful baseball park snuggly in the opening. Tucked away in a small corner of the city, it was a masterpiece of planning and design to create a ballpark that fits so naturally into its surroundings.

10. The Colors

Target Field is beautiful in all respects, and part of the beauty comes from the colors found throughout. From the green grass to the natural limestone to the flashing scoreboard lights, Target Field is a feast for the eyes.

5 BEST THINGS ABOUT METROPOLITAN STADIUM

Metropolitan Stadium in Bloomington was a great ballpark. Most of the seats seemed good. Just looking up at the giant decks surrounding the baselines made you want to go up and try out every seat. What a great view from the very top! Those monster stands in left field just begged for someone to hit a ball to the upper deck. (Harmon finally hit one up there.) The right field bleachers were fan-friendly, and the giant batter's eye in center had all the right makings of a great outdoor stadium. I often think back to games at the old Met, and it was an easy task for me to come up with things I liked about this great ballpark.

1. Home of the Twins
There was something special about just knowing that the ballpark was the home of our Minnesota Twins. It was just simply a beautiful place to watch baseball.

2. The Seats and Sightlines
Even out in the right field bleachers was a good seat. The park had good sightlines, and I enjoyed sitting in different places. If you walked all the way up to the top of the upper deck and looked down, you got a wonderful perspective on the game. I loved the seats up high.

3. Tailgating
There was always something going on in the parking lot before games. It was a huge parking area for baseball and for football when the Vikings were playing.

(Continued)

4. Killebrew Home Runs and the Left Field Upper Deck

I can still see that huge upper deck in left field. It was so ominous, and there was always the anticipation that, during any game, Killebrew might hit one of his gigantic home runs. I think often about the place up in the left field upper deck where Harmon hit his monster home run back in June 1967.

5. Food

There was nothing better than that hot dog and a Coke (later on, a beer) at the ballgame, and the 25-cent frosty malts were the best anywhere. I still have a hard time finding any that compare to the old Met's frosty malt cups.

10 BEST THINGS ABOUT THE METRODOME

1. **A Haven from the Bad Weather**

2.

3.

4.

5.

6.

7.

8.

9.

10.

10 WORST THINGS ABOUT THE METRODOME

This category is an easy one to fill.

1. Parking
Horrible, horrible, horrible for the fans. Not enough spaces, and so often a mess getting in or out.

2. Corridors
Cramped, crowded, and little room to walk. Good luck trying to walk around. Of course, for many years, the crowds at Twins games were sparse and the room was ample, but never for a Vikings game. Plus, you couldn't see the field whenever you went up for food or to use the restrooms.

3. Getting Food or Using the Restrooms
Again, good luck with that. Crowded, long lines—not a good experience.

4. Sightlines
Simply horrible for baseball. Did you ever come home with a crick in your neck? The seats were positioned for viewing football, and in many sections you would have to turn your head or your whole body to see the action on the field.

5. Seating
In addition to the poor sightlines, it also was tough just getting in and out of your seat if you were in the middle of those long, long rows. You felt guilty any time you got up during the game to get something to eat or use the restroom with the number of people that you had to disturb to get out of the row.

6. Indoors
Baseball played indoors. It just isn't right!

7. The Right Field Baggie
Are you kidding me?

8. The Roof
Well, a few fly-pop outs got caught up there. Do I need to say anything else?

9. The Roof, Again
It deserves two spaces on the list. The roof once collapsed, and the Vikings had to play a home game in Detroit. Did I really just say that?

10. The Whole Thing!
Other than some great games and excitement created by the teams who played there, I can't think of much good to say about the Metrodome.

MY FAVORITE BALLPARK FOOD ITEMS

It's quite simple: I like to eat, and I especially like to eat at baseball games. Here's my list of all-time favorites that just fit perfectly at certain ballparks. Enjoy the smells and the tastes just as I have—or try anyway!

1. **Frosty Malts at Metropolitan Stadium**
Anybody who ever devoured the 25-cent malt cups at the old Met Stadium will know why this is number one on the list. I can still remember the taste as they melted in the hot sun. Eating at least a couple of them was standard operating procedure at the ballpark during Twins games.

2. **Hot Dog at Wrigley Field in Chicago**
Maybe it's simply being at Wrigley Field for a Cubs game, or maybe it's just the Chicago-style hot dog, but as far as I am concerned, there is no better taste or look or smell than a hot dog with all the trimmings at Wrigley.

3. **Brats at Target Field**
Now I really am hungry! Save your taste buds and your appetite until you get to Target Field and then have a brat. The flavor is out of this world. It will taste even better if you can wait until you get to your seat and enjoy the view of Target Field while you eat the brat. It's heavenly!

4. **Pizza at Yankee Stadium**
Okay, okay, I had to go all the way to New York and venture into Yankee Stadium to get the best ballpark pizza. But it is the best. Will I have more than one piece? You can count on it.

5. **Target Field Peanuts**
Well, the truth is I love peanuts wherever I eat them, so why not eat them at the most beautiful ballpark in the majors, Target Field?

6. Hot Chocolate

This drink is good anywhere, but on a cold evening at Target Field, it doesn't get any better than that! It's not bad at a football game outdoors either, but I will take a baseball game to warm up the body.

7. Hot Dog at the Old Yankee Stadium

I have to apologize again for going all the way to New York for this, but facts are facts. A hot dog at the old Yankee Stadium was something special. Maybe it was because "The Babe" ate so many of them there. The atmosphere, the crowd, the ambiance, and the memories of Ruth, Gehrig, DiMaggio, and Mantle probably contribute to the appeal.

8. Frosty Malt at the Dome

Okay, I didn't like the Dome, but I do like ice cream, so I guess I will have to add this here. The price wasn't 25 cents like at the old Met but rather $4.50—but they were pretty good.

9. Dome Dog

I'm still at the Dome for this one, but only because I was there so often and those Dome Dogs were pretty good too. They were big, and the fact is I just like hot dogs. I'm not saying that I liked the Dome—just the Dome Dogs.

10. Brats, Cheese, and Anything Else You Want to Eat at Lambeau Field

I know this is a list of the best food at baseball parks, but when thinking of stadium food, I would feel like a fraud if I didn't mention Lambeau Field in Green Bay. Yes, even being a Vikings fan, I have to be honest and say that the food at Lambeau, especially in those historic surroundings, is fabulous.

HOCKEY

10 GREATEST MINNESOTA WILD PLAYERS

The Minnesota Wild have not been around all that long, but in the franchise's first 13 seasons, some great players have donned the skates at the Excel.

1. Marian Gaborik

One of the down days in franchise history had to be when Marian Gaborik left to sign with the New York Rangers in 2009. He had been the Wild's best player, and to date he still ranks as the top goal scorer and point producer in franchise history. The third overall pick in the Entry Draft for the Wild in 2000, the Czech-born winger spent eight years here and was the team leader in goals scored in five of those seasons.

2. Mikko Koivu

Mikko has been a great puck distributor and scorer since joining the Wild in 2005. His abilities and his stature among his teammates have earned him the captain's role. A great playmaker and fan favorite, the burly Finn holds the franchise record for career assists, and he trails only Gaborik in goals scored as of the 2013–14 season.

3. Wes Walz

Wes was a steady and solid player for many years with the Wild. He first came into the NHL as a teenager with the Boston Bruins, and after six seasons with four different teams and then four years in Europe, Wes joined the Wild in their inaugural season, where he remained for seven years. He was instrumental in the team's run to the conference finals in 2002–03. Short-handed goals were one of his specialties.

(Continued)

4. Brian Rolston

Primarily a center, Brian could play all the forward positions and play them well. He spent just three of his 17 NHL seasons in Minnesota, but he was one of the team's top two goal scorers in each of those three seasons. His booming shot from the point on power plays was a treat to watch. As a freshman at Lake Superior State, Brian scored the winning goal in the collegiate hockey championship game.

5. Dwayne Roloson

Dwayne gave us some outstanding years in the net for the Wild and was an exceptionally skilled goalie. After going undrafted out of college, he reached the NHL at the age of 27 with the Calgary Flames before launching an 18-year NHL career. He played in Minnesota for three and a half seasons, during which time he saved nearly 92 percent of the shots against him.

6. Andrew Brunette

Andrew had two three-year stints with the Wild and was an extremely durable player, playing in at least 80 games in each of his six seasons here. He once had a stretch of 509 consecutive games played, for both the Wild and the Colorado Avalanche (where he played between his Wild stints). He had an excellent shot and scored some huge goals for Minnesota, most notably the game-winner in overtime to defeat Patrick Roy and the Avalanche in Game 7 of the 2003 Western Conference Quarterfinals.

7. Brent Burns

Brent was a solid defenseman who could really move the puck up the ice. He was another guy who was tough to see leave when his Wild career came to an end. Brent was drafted by the Wild as a forward in the first round in 2003, when he was 18 years old. Then-coach Jacques Lemaire converted Brent to defense, and it really paid off, as he became the Wild's top defenseman for several seasons before being traded to San Jose in 2011.

8. Ryan Suter

Ryan has been with the Wild only since 2012, but at this point in his career he is clearly one of the best defensemen in all of hockey. After seven seasons with the Nashville Predators, Brian was signed as a free agent to a huge multiyear, multimillion-dollar contract. He went on to lead the Wild in assists and help take them to the playoffs in his first year on the blue line in Minnesota. Ryan's dad played on the gold-winning 1980 U.S. Olympic hockey team.

9. Zach Parise

Zach was another of the Wild's huge free-agent signings prior to the 2012–13 season, along with Suter—the two were signed to identical 13-year, $98 million deals. Parise, who came from the New Jersey Devils, led Minnesota in goals and points in his first season here and further established himself among the top forwards in the NHL. Born in Minneapolis, Zach is the son of J. P. Parise, who played many years for the North Stars in the 1960s and '70s.

10. Niklas Backstrom

Nicklas has served the Wild well in the nets in his eight years with the team and certainly has been one of the franchise's best goalies. The Finnish-born netminder signed with Minnesota in 2006, and while splitting time with Manny Fernandez before taking the full-time job, he led the NHL with a .929 save percentage and 1.97 goals-against average in his first season.

10 GREATEST MINNESOTA NORTH STARS PLAYERS

1. Bobby Smith

Bobby was a complete player. He had the size, skills, and all that it took to be a great player. Bobby began and ended his career for the North Stars, eight years in all, with a seven-year stint with the Montreal Canadiens in between. One of the most popular North Stars players, Bobby led the team in goals and assists as a 20-year-old rookie in 1978–79, and in his third season he helped lead Minnesota to the Stanley Cup Finals. His 114 points scored in 1981–82 stand as a franchise record.

2. Steve Payne

Steve came to the North Stars the same year as Smith and remained with the team for his entire ten-year career before having to retire because of spinal injuries. He was a special player who lit up the net 228 times. Steve scored 17 goals and had 12 assists in the playoffs during the team's run to the Stanley Cup Finals in 1980–81.

3. Dino Ciccarelli

Dino always seemed to find a way to put the puck in the net, and he had a way of playing that could really excite the crowds. He began his NHL career with the North Stars in 1980 and remained with the team for nearly nine seasons, twice scoring more than 100 points in a season. He averaged more than a point per game during his North Stars career, best in franchise history. The Hall of Famer played 19 seasons in the NHL and finished his career with 1,200 points.

4. Mike Modano

One of the all-time greats, Mike Modano played just shy of 1,500 games in his NHL career from 1989 to 2011. His first four seasons were in Minnesota, and he continued to shine when the franchise moved to Dallas, where he won a Stanley Cup title in 1999. The Michigan native holds the NHL record for the most points scored by an American-born player.

5. Cesare Maniago

Cesare seemed to be in the net forever. He was taken with the first pick in the expansion draft by the North Stars in 1967 and then remained a strong and reliable goalie for Minnesota for nine seasons, putting in many minutes on the ice. His 26 shutouts in goal for the North Stars are the most by any netminder while the franchise was in Minnesota.

6. J. P. Parise

J. P. was another fan favorite because of his style as a grinder and hustler. He could always be counted on. Parise was with the North Stars from 1967 until the 1974–75 season, when he was traded to the New York Islanders, with whom he would go on to win two Stanley Cup championships before returning to Minnesota for his final season in 1978–79.

(Continued)

7. Bill Goldsworthy

Watching Bill play was as exciting as it gets. He had the name and the flare and was a solid player. Fans will never forget the "Goldy Shuffle," which he performed after scoring a goal at home. Goldy came to Minnesota from the Bruins in the 1967 Expansion Draft and remained here until 1976. He was a captain for two seasons and had his best year in 1974, when he scored 48 goals. In the playoffs for the 1967–68 season, he scored a team-best eight goals and had seven assists in the team's run to the semifinals.

8. Neal Broten

A two-time NHL All-Star, Neal had all the skills and attitude and was great around the net. The Roseau native and Golden Gophers star was drafted by the North Stars in 1979 and joined the team a year later. His 76 assists in 1985–86 are a single-season franchise record, and his 554 assists in 13 years for the North Stars are the most by anybody while the team was in Minnesota. He was inducted into the U.S. Hockey Hall of Fame in 2000.

9. Brian Bellows

Brian was a highly skilled player who could light up the rink and move the puck. He debuted with the North Stars as an 18-year-old and starred for Minnesota for ten seasons, becoming the franchise's top all-time goal scorer for Minnesota. He later won a Stanley Cup as a member of the 1992–93 Canadiens.

10. Craig Hartsburg

What a great defenseman for the North Stars! A first-round draft pick in 1979, Craig had it all: great skills and a great shot. He was around for 570 games and accumulated more than 300 assists in his career. Since retiring in 1989, Craig has been a head coach in the NHL for Chicago, Anaheim, and Ottawa.

MY FAVORITE MINNESOTA NORTH STARS

Every time I think of the Minnesota North Stars, it still breaks my heart that they left, even after all these years and the arrival of a new NHL franchise in Minnesota. But the North Stars left behind many great memories and people. Here is my list of ten personal favorite players and coaches from North Stars history—and the list could go on and on. I regrettably had to leave off such legendary players as Dino Ciccarelli and Neal Broten, among others. It's still hard, but it takes away some of the pain (see, there's another: Steve Payne) to think back on these great players and personalities.

1. Cesare Maniago

What a goalie! Cesare had it all. He was big and fast and was tremendous in the goal for so many years. The first thing I think of when the North Stars are mentioned is Cesare. I miss him. Nine years he was with us, and he had so many great games, shutting down opponents.

2. Bobby Smith

Bobby was such a great player here for so many years. He was big, strong, and such a smooth player. When he was traded, it was tough to take. It was difficult to see him go, but he wanted to leave. It worked out for Bobby, because he won a Stanley Cup championship with the Montreal Canadiens in 1986.

3. J. P. Parise

J. P. was a true representative of the North Stars. He was a real grinder, a hard worker, and an outstanding person. It is so nice to see his son Zach in uniform for the Minnesota Wild. J. P. never let up throughout his 45 playoff games and 588 regular-season games as a North Star.

(Continued)

4. Lou Nanne

Louie probably should be at the top of this list because of our friendship, his personality, and all the things he did for the North Stars in his roles as player, coach, general manager, and president. There is only one Lou Nanne! He was an excellent player for the North Stars, playing both forward and defense after spending his college career at the U as a defenseman.

5. Glen Sonmor

I don't know anyone who doesn't like Glen Sonmor. His passion and love for the game is beyond anyone's imagination. Glen was an outstanding and committed coach second to none. He had a great hockey career and continued to entertain us as the colorful commentator of Minnesota Golden Gophers hockey for many years. Known as a rough and tough player during his short NHL career, he coached the Gophers and then North Stars three different times, taking the Stars into the playoffs four of the six seasons that he coached.

6. Bill Goldsworthy

Who can ever forget the famous "Goldy Shuffle"? Bill was a great player, a fan favorite, and someone whom I really admired. He could really put electricity into an ice arena.

7. Mike Modano

Mike was one of the best players of his era. He had some outstanding seasons with the North Stars and continued to excel after the team moved to Dallas.

8. Curt Giles

Curt was an excellent defenseman for the North Stars from 1979 to 1991, interrupted by a stint with the Rangers for part of two seasons. He was steady and a strong blue-liner. After his playing career ended, he became a successful high school hockey coach in the Twin Cities.

9. Craig Hartsburg

Craig is another of the great defensemen to play for the North Stars. I always liked his consistency and his ability to move the puck up the ice.

10. Gump Worsley

I got to number ten, and it was so tough to think about all the guys I had to leave off, but I couldn't complete the list without "The Gumper." Lorne "Gump" Worsley was already 40 years old and had established a legendary career with the Rangers and Canadiens by the time he came to the North Stars during the 1969–70 season. He guarded the net for 107 games in Minnesota and was just a great guy to have around on the team. He later became a scout for the North Stars.

10 TOUGHEST NORTH STARS AND WILD PLAYERS

This list isn't just about enforcers and fighters; it's about guys who were tough and played without fear. For this one, I put our two teams, the North Stars and the Wild, together.

1. Derek Boogaard

His was such a tragic death for a gifted young man. Boogaard was a fighter and he was tough. During his entire career, he played the role of the enforcer. At 6-foot-7 and about 260 pounds, he was a real force to be reckoned with.

2. Elmer "Moose" Vasko

Moose came to Minnesota from the Chicago Blackhawks near the end of his career, playing here for two seasons. Most players just stayed away from him on the ice.

3. Zenon Konopka

Keep this guy away from me! Zenon is one tough hockey player and has logged more than 1,000 penalty minutes in less than nine seasons in the NHL. In his first year with the Wild, he collected zero goals and zero assists while leading the team with 117 penalty minutes.

4. Basil McRae

McRae was a tough guy who knew how to rough up others on the ice. He could hold his own most anywhere. In his five seasons with the North Stars (1987–92), this enforcer averaged more than 313 penalty minutes per year, including a franchise-record 382 PIM in 1987–88.

5. J. P. Parise

Remember, this category is not just about fighting but about toughness—and J. P. was one tough hockey player. He was always available when needed, a committed and dedicated player.

6. Wes Walz

Wes could mix it up with the best of them. He was a tough, tough player who also had a great shot.

7. Glen Sonmor

I had to include coach Sonmor, because his reputation as a tough, fierce player came with him to the bench. A man of great passion, he was the impetus behind the big fight in Boston with the North Stars that was the most penalized game in NHL history.

8. Willie Mitchell

Wow! What a fun player to watch, and what a tough guy he was while playing four seasons on the Wild's blue line.

9. Ted Harris

Ted came to the North Stars in 1970 after seven seasons with Montreal, and he brought all the tools with him. He was a solid defenseman and could really mix it up when necessary. He served as team captain during his three years in Minnesota.

10. Tom Reid

Tom was a solid blue-liner with the North Stars for nine and a half seasons. He retired in 1978 at the age of 31 due to a rash caused by the hockey equipment. Tom now serves as an outstanding color commentator for the Wild.

5 BEST THINGS ABOUT XCEL ENERGY CENTER

I like to say that the best thing about watching hockey at the Xcel Energy Center is that there is not a bad thing about watching hockey at the Xcel Energy Center. It is simply a great arena. The seats are tucked in close to the ice. The press box is terrific, and the corridors and food and restroom locations are convenient.

1. Good Seats on Every Level
It is hard to make a case that there's a bad seat at the Xcel. Even in the lower-priced ticket areas, the seating is excellent with great views to the ice surface, and comfortable too.

2. The Atmosphere
Everything about the setting is superb. The pulse in the arena, the music, the crowd noise, the lighting; it's all terrific.

3. Press Box
Even though it is high up in the arena, everything about the press box is positive. It has easy access, good seating, and an excellent place to do game coverage.

4. Scoreboard
The scoreboard is dynamic and does a great job of catching the fans' attention. It is beautifully designed and provides excellent information.

5. The Wild
The Wild are a fun and exciting team, and coming into this great environment to watch them play makes for an enjoyable experience all around. The uniforms and all the various color combinations are also outstanding.

10 GREATEST MINNESOTA GOPHERS HOCKEY PLAYERS

This is definitely another tough category to stop at ten, because there have been so many great Gophers.

1. John Mariucci

You have to be number one on the list when you become a legend and have an arena named after you. John played both football and hockey for the university and then moved on from Gophers hockey to a successful five-year career with the Chicago Blackhawks in the NHL, where he was known as a tough, hard-nosed defenseman. He is probably best remembered for his success as the Gophers' hockey coach in the 1950s and '60s. He was inducted into the U.S. Hockey Hall of Fame in Eveleth as well as the Hockey Hall of Fame in Toronto.

2. John Mayasich

John was maybe the best all-around player in Minnesota hockey history. Like Mariucci, Mayasich was a native of Eveleth on the Iron Range, and he played for Mariucci on the Gophers and on the 1956 U.S. Olympic hockey team. He was also a member of the 1960 Olympic hockey team that won gold. John had been a dominant player for Eveleth High School and was ranked first on the *Star Tribune*'s list of the 100 greatest players in Minnesota high school hockey history. He still holds the U of M records for most career goals and most career assists, and he once scored eight points in a single game against Michigan in 1954—an NCAA Tournament record. A three-time All-American with the Gophers, Mayasich is the only player to have his number (8) retired by the program. He is a member of the U.S. Hockey Hall of Fame.

(Continued)

3. Lou Nanne

Louie was a fabulous defenseman and the first defenseman to win the Western Collegiate Hockey Association scoring title. He was also the WCHA Most Valuable Player in 1963. He served as captain of the Gophers in his senior season, playing under John Mariucci. Lou had all the tools: a great shot and tremendous skills on both the defensive and offensive side. The Ontario native became an American citizen in 1967 and became the captain of the 1968 U.S. Olympic hockey team.

4. Neal Broten

Neal was a great player for Minnesota and went on to tremendous success in his Olympic and professional careers. The oldest of three Broten brothers to come out of Roseau High School on the Iron Range, Neal played for Herb Brooks at the U of M and was named WCHA Rookie of the Year in 1978–79. He scored the game-winning goal in the Gophers' championship-winning victory over North Dakota in the 1979 NCAA Tournament. After playing for Brooks on the gold-medal Olympic team in 1980, Neal returned to the Gophers and won the 1981 Hobey Baker Award as the top nation's collegiate hockey player.

5. Bill Baker

Another strong and highly skilled Gopher, Bill was a tremendous defenseman on the Gophers' varsity team for all four of his years at the U. He was the team captain in 1978–79 and was named a WCHA First Team All-Star for the 1978–79 season. A Grand Rapids native, Bill played with Neal Broten and seven other Golden Gophers for Herb Brooks on the 1980 Olympic team that defeated the Soviets at Lake Placid. After the Olympics, Bill had a brief three-year stint in the National Hockey League.

6. Mike Crowley

Mike had all the skills and abilities, allowing him to shine every time he hit the ice. He was a great player to watch. Hailing from Bloomington, Mike played three seasons for the Gophers and was team captain in 1996–97; he was also the WCHA Player of the Year that season. An exceptional defenseman, Mike was drafted by the Philadelphia Flyers as a high schooler in 1993, and his rights were eventually traded to Anaheim, where he had a brief career in the NHL.

7. Jack McCartan

Jack was a tremendous goalie for the Gophers from 1955 to 1958. He put up a door in the net that rarely opened. The St. Paul native was an All-American at Minnesota as well as a captain of the team during his senior season in 1957–58. He went on to win a gold medal as the goaltender for the 1960 Olympic team at Squaw Valley. Jack was drafted by the New York Rangers in the NHL but couldn't establish a career at that level, spending many years playing pro hockey at the minor league level.

8. Johnny Pohl

Johnny was so much fun to watch. He would take your breath away with his abilities and really light up the arena. Johnny was a captain on the Gophers' 2002 national championship team and was the team's top scorer in both 2000 and 2002. The Red Wing High School product had a brief career in the National Hockey League with the St. Louis Blues and Toronto Maple Leafs.

(Continued)

9. Ken Yackel

Ken is from way back, playing for the Gophers in the early 1950s, but he was one of the best athletes to ever play at Minnesota. He was a highly skilled, tough hockey player who was inducted into the U.S. Hockey Hall of Fame in 1986. He played very briefly in the NHL (only six games for the Boston Bruins) but had a magnificent minor league career, playing for the Minneapolis Millers of the International Hockey League from 1960 to 1963. He also was a member of the 1952 U.S. Olympic hockey team, which took home the silver medal at the Oslo Games.

10. Jordan Leopold

In Jordan's three years with the Gophers in the early 2000s, he was twice named the WCHA Defensive Player of the Year, twice made the WCHA First All-Star Team, and won the Hobey Baker Award as the best player in collegiate hockey in 2002. He also helped the Gophers win a national championship in 2002, the first for the U in more than 20 years. He has since played more than a decade in the NHL.

MY TOP 5 REASONS TO HAVE LUNCH WITH LOU NANNE

1. Then You Won't Have to Have Supper with Him
Just kidding! Louie is a classic, as fun a person as you will ever be around. Having lunch with him any day would be an absolute blast!

2. He Is a Great Storyteller and Conversationalist
With Louie, you don't have to worry about carrying the conversation. He can talk—but he is about as interesting as anyone you will ever talk to. He knows about more things than you can possibly imagine, and believe me, it is all interesting! He'll share stories from his experiences in hockey, his travels all over the world, and his ideas on just about any imaginable subject. He has a story for every occasion. They can be humorous or sad, always filled with passion and exuberance and emotion. He is probably—no, he is definitely—the best storyteller I have ever known.

3. You'll Have a Million Laughs
Louie has a great sense of humor, and I always know that a lunch with him will be chock full of laughs.

4. He Is an Uplifting and Inspiring Person
No matter how good or how bad you may have been feeling that particular day, I guarantee you will feel better after having lunch with Louie. He has a charisma that will lift you up by just being around him. He has a truly inspirational personality. Louie has been a success in hockey and in business, and his boundless energy shows you why. His energy level seems to never diminish. It has to be why he outworked every player that he played against.

5. A Good Time
Just being around Louie is a good time for all.

BASKETBALL

10 GREATEST MINNESOTA TIMBERWOLVES MOMENTS

When I started this section, I was concerned that I wouldn't be able to come up with ten, since the great moments have been few and far between for the Wolves. But once I got started, it was actually quite easy.

1. Getting the Franchise

Clearly, the number one moment in Timberwolves history is the day that the Twin Cities once again became an NBA professional basketball city. The year was 1989. It had been a long time since the Minneapolis Lakers left for Los Angeles (30 years, to be exact).

2. Making the Playoffs in 1997—and Then Seven More in a Row

It did not come easy, but after acquiring Kevin Garnett in the 1995 NBA Draft, the franchise started on a roll a couple years later and made the playoffs for eight consecutive seasons. They had never won more than 29 games in a season prior to the 1996–97 campaign, and then they won 50 or more games four times from 1999–2000 to 2003–04.

3. Drafting Kevin Garnett in 1995

When Kevin came to the Timberwolves, everything changed. He became the nucleus, and the team quickly became a perennial playoff club. KG, taken by Minnesota with the fifth pick, was the first player drafted into the NBA directly out of high school in 20 years.

(Continued)

4. **Defeating Sacramento in the 2004 Conference Semifinals**
This thrilling seven-game series is undoubtedly one of the top
T-Wolves highlights. Capping the best regular-season finish in
franchise history (58–24), the Wolves shed their first-round jinx with
a vengeance, first defeating the Denver Nuggets in the opening
round before defeating Chris Webber's Kings to head to the
conference finals. KG and veteran newcomers Latrell Sprewell and
Sam Cassell led the way for Minnesota.

5. **Drafting Ricky Rubio in 2009**
Wow, what a player! Minnesota and its fans had to wait two
years before Ricky put on a Wolves uniform, while he played out
professionally in his native Spain, but it was worth the wait. If he
can stay healthy, Ricky is going to be a spectacular addition with
his passing and ball-handling abilities.

6. **Kevin Love's 30-30**
It had been nearly three decades since anyone in the NBA had
collected at least 30 points and 30 rebounds in the same game, but
Kevin Love came up with 31 rebounds and 31 points against the
Knicks on November 12, 2010. Incredible! Kevin is a master of the
double-double, and he posted ten 20-20 games that season, but
the 30-30 club is rare company.

7. **49,551 Fans Attend a Timberwolves Game at the Metrodome**
Really?!? Yes, really. In their inaugural season of 1989–90, the
Wolves played their home games at the Metrodome while Target
Center was being built, and more than a million fans attended
games over the course of the season. At the final game, 49,551 fans
showed up. I guess this city can support NBA basketball.

8. 1994 All-Star Game

The Timberwolves hosted the NBA All-Star Game at Target Center in 1994, and it was quite a big deal for the city and another example of how this community is proud and supportive of big-time basketball again. Unfortunately, the woeful T-Wolves didn't have any players in the game.

9. Glen Taylor Buying the Team

When Mankato businessman Glen Taylor bought the team in 1994, he put the franchise on a sound financial footing and helped ensure that it remained in Minnesota. Although the team has struggled on the court for many years, the ownership is solid with Taylor at the helm.

10. Malik Sealy's Game-Winner

Malik actually had two game-winners, but I am referring to the last-second shot he hit to win the December 27, 1999, game against Orlando. His last-second shot a few weeks later on January17, 2000, to beat the Pacers was pretty spectacular too!

10 WORST MINNESOTA TIMBERWOLVES MOMENTS

1. Malik Sealy's Death

May 20, 2000, was a truly sad and tragic day for the Wolves organization, when Malik Sealy was killed in an automobile accident while driving home from a birthday party for Kevin Garnett. The 30-year-old swing player had just completed his eighth NBA season and had established himself as key member of the Wolves' starting lineup. His jersey number 2 has been retired by the Timberwolves.

2. Kevin Garnett Trade

After 12 years as the Wolves' best player and the heart and soul of the franchise, Kevin Garnett was traded to the Boston Celtics following the 2006–07 season. In exchange for KG, Minnesota received up-and-coming center Al Jefferson and four other players, plus two draft picks, but the team fell into a downward spiral for the next several seasons. Garnett, meanwhile, built on his Hall of Fame credentials with Boston and won a long-awaited championship in 2008, his first season as a Celtic.

3. The Joe Smith Contract

When NBA officials learned, after the 1999–2000 season, that the Wolves had made a secret agreement with free agent forward Joe Smith in 1998 promising him a big payday in the future if he would sign for less money at that time, the league came down hard on the organization. Not only was Smith's contract voided, but the NBA took away multiple future draft picks and levied a big fine. While Smith did later re-sign with the team, the former number-one pick contributed little on the court, and the lost draft picks set the franchise back significantly for years to come.

4. Flip Saunders Firing

After taking over as head coach early in the 1995–96 season, Flip Saunders went on to lead the Wolves to eight consecutive playoff appearances, taking them as far as the Western Conference Finals in 2004. But the very next season, with the team struggling around .500, Wolves GM Kevin McHale fired Saunders and installed himself as head coach. Saunders, a former Gophers basketball player (where he was a teammate of McHale's), had been popular with Wolves fans, and his firing was not well received by some. In 2013, Flip was hired back by the Wolves, serving in McHale's old front-office role.

5. Kevin Love's Knuckle Pushups

I've heard of some dumb, freaky injuries to athletes over the years, but when Kevin Love, the team's top star and franchise player, broke his hand while doing knuckle pushups and had to sit out the first three weeks of the 2012–13 season, that was a new one to me.

6. – 10. Draft Busts

Over the course of their first 25 seasons, the Timberwolves have made a few good picks on draft day—Kevin Garnett and Ricky Rubio, to name two—but their legacy of draft busts fills out the list of worst Timberwolves moments. Presented here are the five most regrettable picks, in chronological order.

Gerald Glass: Taken with the 20th pick in the 1990 NBA Draft, Glass lasted for a little more than three seasons in the league, the first two with Minnesota.

Paul Grant: Another 20th overall pick, this one in 1997, netted a player whose pro basketball career was virtually nonexistent. The former Wisconsin Badger played in only 16 NBA games, four of them with Minnesota. (Three picks after Minnesota selected Grant, Seattle drafted former Gopher Bobby Jackson, who went on to have a respectable 12-year NBA career.)

(Continued)

Will Avery: Will was the 14th overall pick by the Wolves in the 1999 NBA Draft. The former Duke Blue Devil played here only three years before being released. No NBA team signed him, and he went overseas to play.

Ndudi Ebi: When the Wolves finally got a shot at a first-round pick after forfeiting their previous three because of the Joe Smith contract fiasco, they used it to take Texas high schooler Ndudi Ebi with the 26th pick of the 2003 draft. The 6-foot-9 forward never developed into the player the team had hoped, and he appeared in just 19 NBA games before departing the league.

Jonny Flynn: The Timberwolves had accumulated four first-round picks in the 2009 draft. They used their first one on European guard phenom Rubio, with the fifth overall selection. With the very next pick in the draft, they took another point guard, Jonny Flynn out of Syracuse University. Although he made the All-Rookie Second Team in 2009–10, Flynn was gone from Minnesota after his second season following hip surgery. He played briefly for Houston and Portland in 2011–12 and is now out of the league entirely. The player taken with the seventh pick in the draft, immediately following Flynn, has emerged as one of the top guards in the NBA: Stephen Curry.

10 GREATEST MINNESOTA TIMBERWOLVES PLAYERS

1. Kevin Garnett

No question about who's number one. Kevin was a dominating player for the Wolves and will go down in NBA history as one of the best ever. In his 12 seasons in Minnesota, he was an All-Star ten times, a First Team All-Defensive selection eight times, a member of the All-NBA First Team three times, and the league MVP in 2003–04. A certain Hall of Famer, KG was also the team's emotional leader, always giving his all, and he was a true fan favorite. He holds many of the team's career records.

2. Stephon Marbury

Some Wolves fans resent the way Steph left Minnesota, but there's no denying that he had two great years here. He could really move the ball up the court and was an excellent passer. He made the NBA All-Rookie Team in 1996–97 while averaging nearly eight assists and 16 points per game. He improved on those numbers in his second year and helped lead the Wolves to the first winning season in franchise history. Unhappy in Minnesota, Marbury demanded a trade and was shipped to New Jersey during the 1999 season.

3. Tom Gugliotta

Tom was an exceptional player and scorer for the Wolves for three and a half seasons. He twice averaged 20 points per game and was a solid rebounder (8.5 boards per game as a Timberwolf) and a great passer for a big man. He spent 13 seasons overall in the NBA.

4. Kevin Love

Since coming to the team in a draft-day trade in 2009, Kevin has quickly emerged as one of the NBA's best players with his superior ability to score and rebound. By his second season, he

(Continued)

averaged a double-double. Love exploded in his third year, when he led the NBA in rebounds, averaged 20 points per game, earned his first All-Star selection, and won the NBA Most Improved Player Award. That season, he also had a streak of 53 consecutive games with at least ten points and ten rebounds, most in the NBA since 1973–74. Showing his versatility, Love won the Three-Point Contest during the 2012 NBA All-Star Weekend.

5. Ricky Rubio

From what we have seen thus far in his brief NBA career, Ricky is a superstar in the making. He came on strong immediately as a backcourt genius for the Wolves in his rookie year of 2011–12, but an ACL tear suffered in March took him off the court for the second half of the season and the beginning of the next. Ricky, who began his pro basketball career as a teenager in Spain (he made his debut when he was just 14), has the playmaking abilities, speed, and defensive skills to become one of the NBA's best, if he can stay healthy.

6. Sam Mitchell

Sam was a member of the inaugural Wolves squad in 1989–90 and established himself as a good all-around player. He was among the team's top scorers and rebounders during the first three seasons, and after spending three years with Indiana, Mitchell returned to Minnesota for the final seven years of his career. The durable forward played in 80 or more games in a season five times for the Wolves and appeared in every game of the strike-shortened 1999 campaign. He was also a team leader and a fan favorite during his T-Wolves tenure. He went on to have a successful career as an NBA coach.

7. Sam Cassell

Sam was here for only two seasons, but he was an instrumental part of the franchise's best season to date, when the Wolves won 58 games and reached the Western Conference Finals in 2003–04. Sam could really bring the crowd to its feet with his shooting skills, and he posted a career-best 19.8 points per game in 2003–04. He also averaged more than seven assists per game that year and played in the only All-Star Game of his 15-year NBA career.

8. Wally Szczerbiak

Wally was an excellent all-around player for the Wolves and a popular one as well. The sixth pick in the 1999 draft, he played in Minnesota for six and a half seasons and was one of the most efficient scorers in team history. He was also a solid rebounder for his position. Wally was named to the 1999–2000 NBA All-Rookie Team and was an All-Star in 2002.

9. Al Jefferson

Al came to the Wolves in the Garnett trade and was expected to be the team's star as kind of a replacement for KG. The big man did well in his three seasons in Minnesota, averaging more than 20 points and ten rebounds per game. Al, who was drafted out of high school by the Celtics in 2004, has continued to compete at an elite level since leaving the Timberwolves.

10. Tony Campbell

It's been a few years, but Tony had great skills and could really shoot the basketball. Another member of the inaugural Wolves team, he was an exciting player to watch and averaged more than 20 points per game in his brief stay here with the Timberwolves (1989–92). His 23.3 points per game in 1989–90 is the third best single-season scoring mark by a T-Wolf to date.

5 GREATEST MINNESOTA LYNX PLAYERS

In their short time in the WNBA, the Minnesota Lynx have had some outstanding basketball players. Here are my top five. The list will grow as the years go by.

1. Lindsay Whalen

A Minnesota homegrown talent, Lindsey has scored more than 4,000 points, dished out more than 1,500 assists, and collected more than 1,000 rebounds in her pro career—becoming only the second player in WNBA history to reach those marks. She led the Lynx to two WNBA titles since her return to Minnesota via trade in 2010 and has been an All-Star in three of her first four seasons with the Lynx. Lindsay, who was perhaps the best Gophers women's basketball player of all time, was drafted with the fourth pick in the first round by the Connecticut Sun in the 2004 draft.

2. Seimone Augustus

Seimone is a four-time All-Star who has been one of the leaders on the Lynx's two championship teams. She won the WNBA Rookie of the Year Award in 2006 and was named MVP of the 2011 WNBA Finals after the team's first title run. She regularly ranks among the league and team scoring leaders. Seimone also won numerous awards during her collegiate career at Louisiana State and was a two-time Olympic gold-medal winner with the U.S. women's basketball team in 2008 and 2012. Despite missing nearly all of the 2009 season and part of 2010 to injuries, Seimone ranks among the franchise leaders in many career scoring categories.

3. Candice Wiggins

Candice was the third overall pick in the 2008 WNBA Draft by the Lynx, and she remained with the team through 2012. Coming off the bench as a rookie, she was named the Sixth Woman of the Year in her first season and then started every game for the Lynx in 2009. Although her 2010 season was cut short by injury, she returned as a key player off the bench as the team reached the WNBA Finals in 2011 and 2012. In a surprise move, Candice was traded to the Tulsa Shock before the 2013 season.

4. Maya Moore

An outstanding collegiate player at the University of Connecticut, Maya was selected by the Lynx with the first overall pick in the 2011 WNBA Draft. In her first year, she averaged 13.2 points per game, leading all rookies, and was named the WNBA Rookie of the Year. She has been an All-Star in two of her first three seasons, playing on a team that has reached the WNBA Finals in each of those years, winning twice.

5. Rebekkah Brunson

Rebekkah joined the Lynx in 2010 after the team that drafted her in 2004, the Sacramento Monarchs, folded. She averaged a double-double in her first season in Minnesota, with 11.3 points per game and 10.3 rebounds per game, and in 2011 she tied a WNBA record by notching six consecutive double-doubles to start the season. A rebounding machine, Rebekkah has been a major part of the Lynx's two championship seasons. She was an All-Star in 2011 and 2013 and a member of the WNBA All-Defensive Team in 2011.

10 BEST REASONS TO GO TO A LYNX GAME

I love going to Minnesota Lynx games at Target Center. The team is fun and exciting to watch, and fans always have a great time.

1. Great Family Atmosphere
It really is a great family atmosphere at the games. Fun for young and old alike!

2. Lindsay Whalen
Just to see Lindsay play the game is worth the price of admission. From Hutchinson High School to the University of Minnesota Golden Gophers and now the Lynx—right here in our own backyard!

3. Great Team
The Lynx have been an outstanding team for the last several seasons, playing great and exciting basketball. If you go, you likely will see a win, something they did nearly 80 percent of the time from 2011 to 2013.

4. No Drinking
All a part of the great family atmosphere.

5. Free Throw Shooting
Yes, they make a lot of their free throws (about a 75-percent rate over the last three years), and that's a good thing.

6. Good, Solid Fundamentals

The Lynx have been noted for their sound fundamentals and spirited play.

7. You Might See Kevin Durant

The NBA superstar might be in attendance to watch his girlfriend, Monica Wright, play for the Wolves.

8. Not Overpaid Athletes

The Lynx players are great athletes who play a professional game of basketball without exorbitant salaries.

9. The Crowd

The fans really get into the games and create incredible energy in the building.

10. Jacket Throwing

You might see Lynx coach Cheryl Reeve throw her jacket. She is truly passionate and dedicated to her job and her team.

10 GREATEST MINNESOTA GOPHERS BASKETBALL PLAYERS

One of the great thrills of watching college basketball through the years has been watching our own Minnesota Gophers play in "The Barn." I have had the good fortune of being able to watch and report on some tremendous players for the Maroon and Gold. It was tough narrowing it down to the ten best, and I had to leave some all-time greats off the list, such as Archie Clark, Dick Garmaker, Bobby Jackson, Chuck Mencel, and Voshon Lenard, among others.

1. Mychal Thompson

There might be some argument as to who should be number one, but I have Mychal at the top of my list. He was such an outstanding player—great shooter and rebounder. He averaged more than 20 points and ten rebounds per game during his college career and was named a First Team All-American and the Big Ten's Most Valuable Player in his senior year. Mychal was the number one overall selection in the 1978 NBA Draft, which gives you an idea of his talent. He was drafted by Portland, where he played for seven seasons, and later won back-to-back NBA championships with the Los Angeles Lakers.

2. Kevin McHale

Kevin was so strong under the basket that he was almost impossible to stop when he got the ball. Such a gifted athlete. He could score, rebound, and play solid defense. The third overall pick in the 1980 NBA Draft, Kevin went on to a Hall of Fame career with the Boston Celtics. The Hibbing native later returned to Minnesota as general manager and, briefly, head coach of the Minnesota Timberwolves.

3. Randy Breuer

Randy was a massive, 7-foot-3 center from Lake City, Minnesota, who played for the Gophers from 1979 to 1983. He went on to become a first-round pick by the Milwaukee Bucks in the 1983 NBA Draft and played 11 professional seasons.

4. Lou Hudson

Lou definitely was one of the best players to ever put on the maroon and gold uniform for Minnesota. Just a great player! I loved to watch Hudson with the ball. They called him "Sweet Lou" because of his smooth jump shot, which he used to average 20.4 points over his three years at the U. As a junior, he put up 23.3 points and 10.3 boards per game. Lou went on to become a perennial All-Star with the Atlanta Hawks in the NBA after being the fourth overall pick in the 1966 draft.

5. Sam Jacobson

Sam was special and a lot of fun to watch. He had a great shot and could take over a basketball game. Jacobson was a member of the Gophers team that went to the Final Four in 1997, and the following year he averaged more than 18 points and five rebounds as a senior. Sam came from Park High School in Cottage Grove, where he was named Minnesota's Mr. Basketball in 1994. He was selected by the Lakers in the first round of the 1998 NBA Draft but played only briefly. He then spent a couple of seasons playing professionally in Europe.

(Continued)

6. Ron Johnson

Ron once scored 60 points in a State High School Tournament game for New Prague in 1956. He carried on his great play and game dominance when he came to the Gophers. One of the best to play here, that's for sure. He was named All-American in 1960 for the Golden Gophers.

7. Jim Brewer

I have a lot of big men on my list, and Jim is no exception. He did so many great things on the court for the Gophers during his time here from 1969 to 1973. While playing for Proviso East High School in Illinois, Jim led his team to four straight state championships. He was also on the U.S. Olympic team that lost the infamous game to the Soviet Union in 1972 when the clock did not start in the last two seconds of the game to allow the Soviets to score the winning basket. With the Gophers, he averaged a double-double for his career (13.5 points, 12.1 rebounds) and then was the second overall pick by the Cleveland Cavaliers in the 1973 NBA Draft.

8. Willie Burton

Willie was so much fun to watch play for the Gophers. He was a true game-changer when he got hot with the ball. He was named All-Big Ten as a senior in 1990 when he averaged 19.3 points per game and helped lead the Gophers to the Elite Eight in the NCAA Tournament. Willie played professionally for several seasons after being drafted by the Miami Heat as the ninth overall pick in 1990. Later, after signing with the Philadelphia 76ers, he scored 53 points in a game against the Heat in 1994.

9. Ray Williams

Ray was such a terrific player. He could really bring the ball up the court, shoot, and play all aspects of the game. He was another player at Minnesota who was a thrill to watch. Ray was the tenth pick by the New York Knicks in the 1997 NBA Draft and played for six NBA teams during his career.

10. Trent Tucker

Trent could easily be higher on the list. He was tremendous in all aspects of the game. A terrific athlete, he brought the crowd to its feet often when he played for the Gophers. Trent played in the National Basketball Association for the New York Knicks and became one of the first three-point specialists in the game. He later played for San Antonio and the champion Chicago Bulls.

10 BEST THINGS ABOUT "THE BARN"

Minnesota Golden Gophers basketball is special because of Williams Arena, affectionately called "The Barn." What a great place to watch college basketball! First built in 1927, it is one of the most distinctive collegiate basketball settings in the country. There have been so many classic games played in this arena and some great players who played for Minnesota. I love the old place!

1. The Raised Floor
The raised playing floor is what gives the arena its charm, makes it different. Remove that, and so much of The Barn's specialness goes away.

2. The Rafters
Just look around the old place, especially way up top. The charm never ends. There is nothing else like it.

3. The Colors
Maroon and gold, bright lights, the brilliant scoreboard—it brightens your spirits and soul. Go Gophers!

4. The "Minnesota Rouser"
When the Golden Gophers come out on the floor and the band plays the "Rouser," chills go up your back. I want to grab a ball and start shooting with the team. The setting, the floor, the rafters, the colors, and then the "Rouser"—it doesn't get much better than that.

5. The Atmosphere
The uniqueness of The Barn and all that goes with it brings about an atmosphere that cannot be equaled.

6. Coziness

The Barn is cozy—some might say "cramped"—and when the house is full and the Gophers are playing well, be sure to bring your earplugs!

7. Public Address Announcer

Dick Jonckowski, the longtime voice of Gophers basketball, sets the tone with his voice, his style, and his passion for the Minnesota Gophers. His voice reverberates and echoes all throughout The Barn.

8. The Food

I don't know if it's just the surroundings and the environment, but the food at The Barn always seems to taste extra good. How could it not taste good with the noise, the atmosphere, the crowd, the uniqueness of the building, and all that comes with Williams Arena and Golden Gophers basketball?

9. The Band

When the band bellows the "Rouser" at The Barn, there are not many places you'd rather be. The sound in the small arena is deafening, and when the band is playing at full peak, it feels like you can hear every instrument on its own. The sounds of the drums, the trumpets, the tubas, and the rest, well, it is just something else.

10. The Students

The U of M students are always rabid supporters of Golden Gophers basketball, but when the team is winning, again, bring some earplugs!

WRESTLING

MY ALL-TIME FAVORITE WRESTLERS

My interest in professional wrestling goes way back to my early days at WCCO television when the pro wrestlers used to come into the studio to do sound bites for the upcoming matches. The sport was so great to watch, and the wrestlers were not only incredible athletes but also great characters and actors as well. There were many and still are, but here are my favorite ten of all time.

1. Verne Gagne

A Minnesota native and local favorite, Verne has to be number one on my list. His promotions of the sport and his championships put him in the fan-favorite and most-popular categories. He won more world heavyweight championships in the American Wrestling Association than any other wrestler (ten). He also played football and wrestled for the University of Minnesota.

2. The Crusher

There will never be another "Crusher." Born Reginald Lisowski, he was one of the greatest wrestlers and actors the sport will ever know. One time, he came on TV with a tire track across his forehead and claimed that Verne Gagne had run him down with his car. Nobody holds more AWA world tag team championships than the Crusher.

3. "Mad Dog" Vachon

I once saw him on a sound bite building a coffin for Verne Gagne. Nobody was better for dramatics. In 1979, he teamed up with Verne on a world tag team championship, and he won five AWA heavyweight titles as an individual.

(Continued)

4. Wilbur Snyder

Wilber was a fan favorite and certainly one of my all-time favorites. He had it all—the build, the clean look, and great athleticism. He once teamed with Gophers football star and future Pro Football Hall of Famer Leo Nomellini to win an AWA world tag team championship.

5. Doctor X

How we loved to hate Doctor X. Also known as "The Destroyer" during his career, Dick Beyer could really draw big crowds for his matches as Doctor X.

6. Kenny Jay

"The Sod Buster," Kenny Jay was another local Minnesotan who was big in the American Wrestling Association. I don't think Kenny ever won a match. He was always on the brink of victory before being flattened at the end.

7. Mitsu Arakawa

Another of the greats who fans loved to hate. He teamed up with Dr. Moto to win the AWA world tag team championship in 1967.

8. Nick Bockwinkel

No doubt, Nick was a big favorite of mine. He had all the wrestling and acting ability that any wrestler would ever want. He won his first AWA world heavyweight championship at the age of 40, in 1975, ending Gagne's long reign.

9. Greg Gagne and Jim Brunzell

This local tag team known as the "High Flyers" was a big fan favorite in the Twin Cities and around the world for many years. Both Greg and Jim still live in the Twin Cities. Greg's father, Verne, was his trainer.

10. Andre the Giant

Andre was special. He was apparently a wonderful person and a great fan favorite. Over 7 feet tall and weighing in at more than 500 pounds, he was so incredibly big that in some ways you almost felt sorry for him. But he brought so much to the sport. Sadly, he died at the young age of 46.

MORE OF
MY
FAVORITE
THINGS

10 GREATEST MINNESOTA OLYMPIC ATHLETES

We have had some great Olympic athletes from the state of Minnesota. As enjoyable as the Olympics are to watch, it becomes even more of a special event when we are able to see our home-state athletes do well. I have had many thrills watching them, and here are my top ten.

1. Neal Broten

After his great years in Minnesota in high school and with the Gophers, Neal's role on the U.S. Olympic team in 1980 puts him at number one on my list.

2. Billy Christian

Another favorite hockey player makes my top ten. A Warroad native, Billy helped lead the U.S. hockey team to the gold medal at Squaw Valley in the 1960 Winter Olympics. He was inducted into the U.S. Hockey Hall of Fame in 1984, and his son Dave played on the 1980 Olympic hockey team.

3. Roger Christian

Like his younger brother Billy, Roger Christian had so many incredible skills. What a treat to watch the two Warroad boys play. Roger was also on the 1960 Olympic hockey team and made the team again in 1964. He joined his brother in the Hall of Fame in 1989.

4. Jack McCartan

The goalie on the 1960 gold medal team also makes it in the top five on my list. Jack also was a great player at the U of M before joining the Olympic team.

(Continued)

5. John Mayasich

Yep, I'm still on hockey here with maybe the best all-around Minnesota-grown hockey player of all time. He played on both the 1956 and 1960 Olympic teams.

6. Cindy Nelson

Cindy was such a great skier and athlete; she brought us a lot of thrills on the slopes. She won the bronze medal at the 1976 Olympics and the silver medal in 1980. She also competed in the 1984 Games and was supposed to be on the 1972 team, when she was just 17, until a hip injury sidelined her just two weeks before the Olympics began. She was born and raised in Lutsen, where her parents ran the local ski area.

7. Amy Peterson

Amy, from St. Paul, was a great Olympic short-track speed skater who competed in five consecutive Winter Olympic Games, from 1988 to 2002. She won a silver medal in 1992 and two bronze medals in 1994. In the 2002 Games in Salt Lake City, she carried the flag at the opening ceremonies. Amy was so special and so much fun to watch.

8. Briana Scurry

Briana was so good in the net for the U.S. national women's soccer team. I was shocked when any team scored against her. She was the goalie on the 1996 gold medal-winning team, allowing a total of just three goals in five matches, and again led the United States to gold in 2004. Briana was a sensational athlete who recorded more than 70 shutouts during her career in international play. She also helped lead Anoka High School to a state championship in 1989.

9. Bill Baker

I'm back to hockey and the incredible "Miracle on Ice" team of 1980. If Bill had not scored a game-tying goal against Sweden in the final seconds during the 1980 U.S. Olympic team's opening game, there would never have been a game against the Soviets or against Finland for the gold medal. He was such a big contributor to the team's success.

10. Mike Ramsey

Still on hockey with Mike Ramsey. Such a great player, Mike was the youngest member of the 1980 Olympic team. Before winning gold in Lake Placid, he starred for Roosevelt High in Minneapolis and then for the Golden Gophers. He had all the skills and will always be one of my favorites. Mike later went on to become an assistant coach with the Minnesota Wild.

5 GREATEST MINNESOTA FEMALE ATHLETES

Over the years, we have watched in amateur and professional sports some outstanding female athletes from Minnesota. They have starred on our local high school and collegiate scenes, on the U.S. Olympic teams, and in professional leagues. Here are my five best of all time.

1. Lindsay Whalen

Lindsey is at the top for two reasons: her tremendous and unrelenting skills as a basketball player at the University of Minnesota and with the Minnesota Lynx, and her tremendous popularity as a player and as a special person.

2. Patty Berg

Patty Berg's prowess on the golf course is remarkable. She won 27 tournaments as an amateur and 57 professional tour events. The Minneapolis native was named Woman Athlete of the Year by the Associated Press in 1938, 1942, and again in 1955.

3. Lindsey Vonn

Lindsey is the face of skiing in the United States. She is one of only three skiers in history to capture four World Cup championships, winning three in a row in 2008, 2009, and 2010 and then again in 2012 after finishing a close second in 2011. She also won gold in the downhill at the 2010 Winter Olympics. Born in St. Paul and raised in Bloomington, Lindsey has been skiing since she was two years old.

4. Cindy Nelson

Cindy was an outstanding skier and was on skis before the age of three. She is the first American to win the downhill in the World Cup. Cindy retired in 1985 with six World Cup event wins.

5. Briana Scurry

Briana was an all-state player in basketball and the National Goalie of the Year in soccer as a senior at Anoka High School. She went on to star as soccer goalie on the 1996 and 2004 Olympic teams.

MY FAVORITE SPORTS CITIES OUTSIDE MINNESOTA

I have traveled to a lot of cities covering sports events during my four-plus decades with WCCO television. Here is a list of my all-time favorite cities where I have covered games or events. To me, great sports cities are those that have nice ballparks and arenas, enthusiastic and friendly fans, and other attractions that make a visit to the city something that I look forward to.

1. New York

The Big Apple is at the top, and of course it has a lot to do with the original Yankee Stadium. The old stadium has been replaced, but I still get chills thinking about walking into "The House That Ruth Built." There was so much history there, and the ambiance— well, just everything about it was special! Throw in the legendary Madison Square Garden for basketball and hockey, and New York is without a doubt the greatest sports stage in the world.

2. Boston

Talk about sports history! Boston has it all. The Celtics, the Bruins, the Red Sox, the Patriots; Bill Russell to Larry Bird, Bobby Orr to Ray Bourque, Ted Williams to Pedro Martinez, John Hannah to Tom Brady. The list goes on and on! And with historic Fenway Park and the old Boston Garden, I love going to cover a game in Boston. Since 2000, no city has won more championships in the big four sports than Boston. And now that the Red Sox have won those multiple World Series championships, they can't complain about the "Curse of the Bambino" anymore.

(Continued)

3. Chicago

Another terrific sports city with all the frills and thrills. We all know about the Cubs and their history, and then we have the White Sox, Blackhawks, Bears, and Bulls. I can only begin with those famous names—Ernie Banks, Bobby Hull, Dick Butkus, Walter Payton, Michael Jordan—a great sports town! It is truly a "love to hate" town for Minnesota fans, but a wonderful place to visit.

4. Pittsburgh

Whenever I think of this city, the "blue collar" concept hits me hard. They have it all with the Pirates, the Penguins, and the Steelers. Remember the amazing "Steel Curtain" defense of the 1970s, and how about Franco Harris and Terry Bradshaw? While it's been a rough couple of decades for the Pirates and their fans, things are getting exiting again for the Bucs, and the Steelers and Penguins have had some great teams and players in recent years. The fans are truly loyal and passionate for their teams, and it's just a great, great city!

5. Philadelphia

Remember Rocky running up those steps? Yep, it was right there in Philadelphia, the City of Brotherly Love. A great sports town with incredible history—"Dr. J," Mike Schmidt, Reggie White, Bobby Clarke, and the "Broad Street Bullies." Such passionate fans; they even once famously booed Santa Claus at an Eagles game!

6. San Francisco

I love going to San Francisco. The beautiful City by the Bay has enjoyed some truly legendary athletes, such as Willie Mays and Joe Montana. There is so much to do in San Francisco, so much to see, and covering sports there—the Giants and the 49ers—is the icing on the cake.

7. St. Louis

With St. Louis, the first thing that comes to my mind is those classic Cardinals baseball uniforms and Stan "The Man" Musial. There is that great statue of Stan right outside the ballpark; it gives you goose bumps just walking by it. The Cardinals have had some great teams over the years. The city has the famous Arch, great restaurants, and beautiful stadiums. I love St. Louis.

8. Denver

Denver has all the beauty one could ask for, with the Rocky Mountains right in its backyard. Just like the Vikings are the heart and soul of the Twin Cities, the Broncos are truly beloved in Denver. Just bring up the city name and right away you think of those old Denver Broncos orange jerseys and John Elway, Floyd Little, and so many more great names. Although the Rockies don't have so long a history in the Mile High City, Coors Field is a great ballpark. And the Avalanche have brought home two Stanley Cup championships in their short time in the city.

9. Green Bay

I know, I know. How could I like any city that houses the hated Green Bay Packers? But Green Bay is such a great sports town and great community, and they really love their Packers. The atmosphere there on game days is unlike anywhere else. The fans parking in driveways and walking to games is historic. And Lambeau Field, you don't have to say anything else. And of course, there was Lombardi too.

10. Madison

Now, I am going to really be chastised by my Minnesota readers, but Madison on game-day Saturdays in the fall is special. Badgers football is filled with such great tradition that it is definitely one of the best places to cover college football. As far as towns with a great atmosphere on Saturday afternoons in the fall, I'll throw in several more too: South Bend, Columbus, and Ann Arbor.

10 BEST SPORTS REASONS TO LIVE IN THE TWIN CITIES

We are so blessed to have all the sports activities that are available to us in the Twin Cities. Few other cities can claim five upper-echelon professional teams, a major Division I university, all the great small college teams, and vibrant prep programs. But it is so much more than that. Our teams are part of the very fabric of the community, with fans as passionate as in any American city—from all the purple-and-gold wearing supporters on Sundays and those clad in maroon and gold on Saturdays to perhaps the most rabid hockey fans in the country, from grade school level right up to the Wild. With TCF Bank Stadium and a new Vikings complex on the way, the state-of-the-art Xcel Energy Center and spectacular Target Field, the charged atmospheres at "The Barn" and Mariucci Center, all the way to the St. Paul Saints' Midway Stadium (where fun is good!) and packed-to-the-gills high school gymnasiums, you don't have to go far to find vibrant and exhilarating sporting events at premier stadiums and arenas. And if you can't make it to the game, there is no shortage of restaurants or sports bars where you can cheer on the local squad with neighbors and fellow fans throughout the metro area and the state.

1. – 6.
We can argue the order to some extent, although the Vikings will always claim the top spot, with the Twins, Wild, Timberwolves, Lynx, and Golden Gophers filling the other five places, in whatever order suits your preference. But in an area with teams representing the NFL, Major League Baseball, the NHL, the NBA, the WNBA, and the Big Ten, you find great tradition and history—although we could use a few more championships.

7. College Football
Beyond the Division I University of Minnesota Golden Gophers, a number of small colleges have proud football traditions in the

Twin Cities, with the University of St. Thomas probably at the top of the list. A little farther afield, you have the Saint John's University Johnnies, in Collegeville, where coach John Gagliardi built one of the most successful programs in the history of Division III football.

8. High School Athletics

Local teams and athletes have excelled at the high school level in the Twin Cities as well, and the football Prep Bowl, the Minnesota State High School Basketball Tournament, and the State High School Hockey Tournament are among the most popular and exciting sporting events year after year. Beyond those big three sports, Minnesota high schools have produced elite talent in numerous other sports, such as soccer, baseball, track and field, tennis, and more.

9. Coaches and Players

Minnesota has always strived to have top athletes and quality people make up our programs at all levels of competition. The Minnesota State High School League has set high standards and governed extremely well over the years to set the bar high for schools, coaches, and players at all levels.

10. Weather

Yes, Minnesota weather provides us with some beautiful fall and spring periods, when watching outdoor sports is incredible. With Target Field in spring and TCF Bank Stadium in fall, it doesn't get much better than that! Sure, we get some pretty bad weather around here—and Minnesotans aren't shy about complaining about the bad weather—but at least in the depths of winter, we can go inside and catch great hometown sports at "The Barn," Xcel Energy Center, Target Center, and other arenas and schools.

MY FAVORITE MINNESOTA SPORTS EVENTS TO COVER

I cover sports for a living. It's what I always wanted to do, and it has been an incredible career. Here are the events that I love to cover the most. I look down the list, the variety of events, and I know that each was special in so many ways. But a Vikings playoff game, well, that has to be at the top of the list!

1. Minnesota Vikings Playoff Game

It didn't seem to matter if the Vikings were involved in a playoff game at old Metropolitan Stadium or the Metrodome; the atmosphere has always been electric. The anticipation and the surroundings make the hours leading up to the game like that at no other event that I have covered. The Twin Cities are great for all of our sports teams, and the Timberwolves, Wild, and Twins are much beloved. But make no mistake about it, this is a Vikings town, and a playoff game for the Purple is like no other event.

2. Minnesota Golden Gophers Football

I love the Gophers, so just being at a Gophers game is special. From the old days of walking down University Avenue with my dad as a kid and going up the ramp into Memorial Stadium, it didn't get much better than that. It wasn't so great in the dome for all those years, but now with Gophers football back on campus at TCF Bank Stadium, the atmosphere has returned.

3. Minnesota State High School Hockey Tournament

The days of covering the tournament on WCCO television with Herb Brooks and Lou Nanne will always have a special place in my heart. The tournament has changed somewhat now with the divisions, but it is still one of my favorite times of the year and one of my favorite places to be. Just to see these kids playing their hearts out from all over the state is really a great thrill.

4. Minnesota Golden Gophers Hockey

The history, the great players of the past—wow, what wonderful memories. At the new Mariucci Arena, Gophers hockey is really something special, and the atmosphere is incredible. The Minnesota hockey fans are passionate, loud, and electric, making it a great place to be in winter.

5. Minnesota Golden Gophers Basketball

Just walking into "The Barn" (even if there is no game going on) can give you chills. There is no basketball arena like it in the world. With the raised floor and the great history, there are not many better places to attend a game. When I think of Gophers basketball, I think of some of the great coaches of the past such as John Kundla, Bill Musselman, Jim Dutcher, and others. And the players, well, there have been so many special ones over the years!

6. Minnesota Twins at Target Field

I loved to go to Twins games at Metropolitan Stadium. I saw Killebrew and Allison, Oliva and Carew, and all the Twins heroes of the past playing outdoor baseball, and it made so many memories from my childhood. The Dome spoiled the experience of Twins games for many years, but now we have Target Field, maybe the greatest ballpark in the major leagues. Win or lose, being at Target Field is enough. What an incredible experience. A super ballpark in every way.

(Continued)

7. Basketball at Any High School Gym

I love high school basketball, and I don't care where I'm covering a game or if I'm just there to enjoy it. The teams, the kids, the parents, the gymnasiums—it is the best! And if the game is close, you better get your earplugs out.

8. Minnesota Wild Playoff Game

Pretty much any Minnesota Wild game at Xcel Energy Center is an experience. It is a beautiful arena, and the atmosphere is unbelievable. But a playoff game, well, it's almost indescribable. A chill runs up and down your back almost from the time you walk in. It is a great place to be during a playoff game—one of my favorites!

9. Minnesota Timberwolves Game

I guess I just like basketball—high school, college, and professional. I know the Wolves haven't given us much of a product to cheer for during a lot of their history, but I enjoy the games anyway. Target Center is a fine place to watch basketball, and being at the games, win or lose, is still special for me.

10. Minnesota Lynx Game

I really enjoy watching the Lynx play. They could be playing a game at a local playground and I would go and watch them. The team is special, the players are so talented, and the games are exciting. They have me hooked, and, no doubt, one of my favorite places to be is at a Minnesota Lynx basketball game at Target Center.

MY BUCKET LIST OF SPORTING EVENTS TO COVER

I have been around the sports scene for many decades covering a variety of sporting events, but there are a few that I have not had the opportunity to cover. These are the ones I would most like to experience.

1. **U.S. Open Tennis Championships**
I would be like a kid at Disneyland if I could get an opportunity to cover the matches at the men's or women's U.S. Open. I really enjoy tennis, either playing or watching, so this would be special to cover.

2. **British Open Golf Championship in Scotland**
Wow! All the history over there, and the atmosphere must be out of this world. I love to play golf (although I never get as much time to do so as I would like), and I really enjoy watching, especially the major tournaments. Just to be in Scotland covering the British Open would be a true highlight of my career.

3. **The Masters**
Augusta National, Bobby Jones, Ben Hogan, the Hogan Bridge, Hogan's double eagle, Nicklaus, Palmer, Player, Woods, Mickelson, the Eisenhower Tree. Where does the history and tradition end? I want to go!

(Continued)

4. The Finals at Wimbledon

Back to tennis again. This is another event that I would love to be at someday. I can't imagine what it must be like at the All England Club in summer. I can see myself sitting there taking in all the action and atmosphere. I hope the opportunity is not too far away.

5. The Kentucky Derby

The history, the music, the crowds, and the moments leading up to the race—plus all those great horse-racing movies—the Kentucky Derby has it all. Someday I will be there. It would add a little if I happened to own the winning horse too—not going to happen!

MY WISH LIST OF MINNESOTA SPORTING EVENTS

Now, having said what my bucket list looks like, this is my wish list of results I'd like to see and cover someday.

1. Minnesota Golden Gophers Winning the Rose Bowl

It has been over 50 years, and I am getting impatient. I want the Gophers to win the Big Ten title so badly, I can hardly stand it. I want to see our Maroon and Gold out there in Pasadena at the Rose Bowl and come home victorious. What a great day that would (will) be!

2. Minnesota Vikings Winning the Super Bowl

I want to be there wherever and whenever it is, whomever they are playing. Doesn't matter the day or night, the day of the week, or the time. I want to be there when the Minnesota Vikings win the Super Bowl!

3. Minnesota Twins Winning the World Series—Again

With the way the past few seasons have gone for the Minnesota Twins, I want so badly for them to start winning again, advance to the playoffs, make it to the World Series, and yes, win it all again. The 1987 and 1991 championships were a long time ago, and I hope to experience that feeling again someday.

4. Minnesota Timberwolves Winning the NBA Championship

I hope I am not dreaming here, but it would be such a special event to be at and to report on. "Timberwolves Finally Win It All." Can't you just see the headlines? I guess that's what dreams are made of.

5. Minnesota Wild Winning the Stanley Cup

I think we all see this as a possibility someday with the young team of exceptional players they have right now. I just hope it's not too far away, because I want to be there when they do it. It will be a special event to be at, and hopefully it will be right here at the X.

5 THINGS THAT NEED TO GO AWAY FROM SPORTS

As much as I love sports and going to sporting events, there are a few things that bother me as a fan. I'm probably not alone in this. See if these things are as bothersome to you as they are to me.

1. The Wave
There should be a severe penalty for whoever started the wave. It is definitely an annoying nuisance when you're trying to watch a game.

2. Artificial Noise Pumped In
Are you kidding me? We have to have noise pumped in to make it sound like the fans are into the game?

3. "This is a Golden Gopher . . . First Down!"
I'm not a big fan of this cheer at the Gophers' football games.

4. Scoreboard Prompts to "Make Noise"
Like with artificial noise, if the game isn't enough to get the fans excited, something else is wrong.

5. Commercialization of Broadcasts
We now have, on a regular basis, things like "First downs are brought to you by . . ." or "This extra point is brought to you by . . ." Come on now, isn't this just a little too much?!

MY 10 FAVORITE TEAM UNIFORMS

I have spent the better part of four decades watching all sorts of teams perform. There has been football in the fall, hockey and basketball in the winter, and baseball in the spring. I have watched these primary sports with teams at all levels—high school, college, and professional—and I have admired the varied uniforms teams have worn. Some have stood out as my all-time favorites.

1. Los Angeles Dodgers

What looks better than the iconic Dodger blue on a baseball player? Seeing my hero Sandy Koufax in the best uniform ever made it all even better. The classic design and distinctive color put it number one on my list.

2. St. Louis Cardinals

Every time I think about the bat, the Cardinals logo, and the colors on the front, I get chills. It has to be one of the all-time great designs. And when Stan "The Man" Musial put on that uniform, well, that was something to talk about and remember forever.

3. New York Yankees

Think about all those legends who fit so nicely in Yankee pinstripes: Ruth and Gehrig and DiMaggio followed by Mantle and Maris and Ford and Berra, right up through Derek Jeter and Mariano Rivera. Nothing else needs to be said.

(Continued)

4. Chicago Cubs

Maybe it is the blue scheme or the logo, or maybe it is just the fact that it's the Chicago Cubs. I mean, how can you not like the Cubs? (Unless you're a Cardinals or White Sox fan, of course.) If they ever do win the World Series, it likely will all change. But for now, we just like the uniform of the perennial losers.

5. USC Trojans Football

Can't you picture Marcus Allen running down the sidelines in that Trojans uniform with the Trojan horse close behind? Maybe it's the atmosphere, the winning tradition, the history, and the Los Angeles Coliseum all packed in together. I don't know for sure, but the uniform contributes to a big part of that appeal.

6. Los Angeles Rams

I suppose having Deacon Jones wearing the old Rams uniform didn't hurt. Or Roman Gabriel dropping back to pass with the big ram horns on the side of his head. That was mighty good too. They were great, colorful uniforms, and the "Fearsome Foursome" made them even more special.

7. Montreal Canadiens

I can't deny that the incredible Montreal teams of the past must have had an influence on my feeling about the uniforms. As I think about them, I see "Rocket" Richard and all the other great Canadiens skating up the ice. Great teams, great uniforms.

8. Oakland Raiders

Al Davis and his infamous Oakland Raiders were something else. Their logo, the silver and black—they were made for intimidation. The tough, gritty players they had in the old days under Davis and coach John Madden didn't exactly hurt the image either. But the uniforms, wow!

9. Boston Red Sox

The history of Fenway Park, the atmosphere, and all that goes with that make the Red Sox uniforms stand out, and that's okay too. Maybe it's the fact that Ted Williams and Carl Yastrzemski wore the Boston uniform, the design, the colors, and all that. The Red Sox uniform is one of the best.

10. Boston Celtics

We're staying in Boston for the last uniform on my top ten of all time with the green shamrock of the Boston Celtics. What a uniform! Again, look who wore it—such greats as Bill Russell, Bob Cousy, and other legends who contributed to all of those championships. Players and championships alone are not the lone criteria for this list, but it helps.
And I just love the Celtic green!

MY 5 LEAST FAVORITE TEAM UNIFORMS

I suppose if I give you my favorite uniforms, I have to also at least acknowledge those that I hate to even look at or think about. Actually, there are more that compete for top billing than these five.

1. Seattle Seahawks
When they wore the all-pewter jersey and pants combo, it was bad, bad, bad. I often thought about changing the channel whenever I saw that color combination.

2. All-Maroon Minnesota Gophers Football
The color isn't so bad—in fact, I like maroon—but when they go all-maroon, head to toe, I just don't like it. They have so many options with the white, the gold, and the maroon; they need to change it up a bit. I really like the maroon jerseys and the gold pants, or going all gold is good too. I don't mind the maroon jerseys with white pants either. Just not the maroon on maroon.

3. Chicago Bears
Actually, the Bears uniforms aren't really that bad. I just don't like the Chicago Bears, so I don't like seeing players wearing that uniform. And yeah, I could say the same thing about the Green Bay Packers and their uniforms too.

4. Houston Astros
There is something about the colors and the star logo from those garish uniforms from the 1970s and '80s. I just don't like them. The new ones aren't too bad, but those old ones—ugh!

5. Toronto Blue Jays
I guess I could make the list much longer than five as I think about it, but I know I don't like Toronto's uniforms. They don't have much imagination.

MY 10 FAVORITE INTERVIEWS

Through more than 40 years in the broadcasting business, I have had the opportunity to interview some incredible athletes. I may have missed some legends, but after a lot of thought and reflection, here are my top ten.

1. Sandy Koufax

The great Dodgers left-hander was my biggest hero growing up, and I was able to interview him when he was here for the 1985 All-Star Game. It was quite the thrill, and he was sensational. I was not disappointed.

2. Harmon Killebrew

I had Harmon on my show, *Rosen Sports Sunday*, many times, and he was always the best. I recall interviewing him after he hit his 500th home run, and as always, Harmon was so humble and gracious.

3. Ted Turner

What an interview I had with the controversial owner of the Atlanta Braves baseball team in 1984. It was unbelievable! He is a character and was a super interview. I could have stayed with him for hours and just listened.

4. Kirby Puckett

Any time that you had the opportunity to interview Kirby, you knew it would be a good time. He could really talk and talk and talk and always had something interesting to say.

5. Randy Moss

If Randy was on, he was a great interview. If not, he was a really bad interview. He made my list of worst interviews too!

(Continued)

6. Billy Gardner

I always enjoyed the opportunity to interview Billy when he was the Twins' manager during the early and mid-1980s. He knew baseball and was fun to talk with about all kinds of things.

7. Jerry Burns

I love Jerry Burns. "Burnsie" is a fantastic person, he knows football, and he can really give you good and interesting conversation.

8. J. R. Rider

Isaiah "J. R." Rider was at times a really good player for the Timberwolves in the early days of the franchise, and he was also quite the character. He had a stormy time here and elsewhere in his NBA career, but I always enjoyed interviewing him.

9. Charles Barkley

The basketball Hall of Famer and now network broadcaster has quite the dynamic personality, which makes him a great character to interview. It was a real treat to talk with Charles.

10. Billy Martin (When He Was with the Yankees)

Billy was not the best person to talk with in the years that he coached and managed with the Twins, but later, when he came to Minnesota while he was manager of the Yankees, I loved to talk with Billy. He always gave me great material.

MY 5 WORST INTERVIEWS

As I have said many times before, I have had the opportunity to be around and interview some great sports people. Most have been wonderful interviews. Some have not. Here are my top five worst interviews. I'm glad there were not more.

1. Woody Hayes

The former Ohio State football coach tops my list. He was arrogant and disinterested, and he never even made eye contact. I guess he was bored with me or something. It was not any fun.

2. Willie Mays

It was early in my career, and I was interviewing the great Willie Mays. I take some of the blame because I was probably not the best interviewer at the time. I asked him a question about interleague play, and his response was not one to lead the sports news that evening. He felt that kind of question should be left for the commissioner's office and not him during an interview.

3. Bobby Knight

Bobby always wanted to control the interview, and I must say, he did. He was difficult to talk to and not much fun to be around from the media's perspective.

4. Randy Moss

Randy made both of my lists: best and worst. When he was off, you just did not want to be around him; not a fun time.

5. Dennis Green and Christian Laettner

I have a tie here for last place. Neither person was one I enjoyed talking with for a variety of reasons. Green was tough to get anything out of and never wanted to say anything specific. Laettner was just not a very nice person to be around.

TOP 5 MINNESOTA SPORTSWRITERS

1. Sid Hartman

No one will ever accomplish what this great iconic figure has done here in the Twin Cities. Even into his 90s, Sid is still at the top of the sports scene. His passion and love for the local teams—especially the Gophers teams—is unequaled.

2. Charley Walters

Charley has been writing his column, "Shooter," for many decades, and he writes an interesting and well-laid-out column in the *Pioneer Press* with pertinent and updated information. Another great sports contributor to his readers and fans.

3. Jim Klobuchar

Jim has been a legendary sportswriter in the Twin Cities going way back to his covering the Minnesota Vikings during the stormy days under head coach Norm Van Brocklin.

4. Dick Cullum

Dick was a longtime and excellent sportswriter in the Twin Cities. He was one of the original columnists with the Minneapolis *Star Tribune* in the 1960s and 1970s.

5. Doug Grow

Doug held the reputation for many years as an outstanding writer and journalist for the *Star Tribune*.

MY 5 FAVORITE STADIUM/ARENA ANNOUNCERS

1. Bob Casey
Bob was the longtime public address announcer for the Minnesota Twins, 44 seasons in all. What a voice! Remember, "No smoking. No smoking in the Metrodome." How about this one: "Now batting for the Twins, Kirrrrrbyyyy Puckett!" Bob was a gem!

2. Jules Perlt
Jules was the longtime voice and public address announcer of Gophers football and basketball. He was one of the best ever. His voice was unbelievable. "Annnnnnnderson in for Minnesota." He was famous for often announcing the score of critical games backwards: "Final score Michigan 3, Iowa 6."

3. Dick Jonckowski
Dick is the current voice of Gophers basketball and baseball on the public address. He has great voice, passion, and love for the Gophers, which brings it all together.

4. Marsh Nelson
The stadium announcer for the Minnesota Vikings for many years, Marsh was absolutely electric with his voice as it reverberated around the stadium. He was a great one.

5. Rod Trongard
Rod was a public address announcer for the Minnesota Fighting Saints hockey team and the Minnesota Kicks soccer club. He also did a lot of play-by-play on radio for several local teams.

MY TOP 5 PLAY-BY-PLAY ANNOUNCERS

This is a tough one to rank because we have been blessed with so many great game callers. Here are my top five.

1. Ray Christensen

When Ray retired and left the airwaves in 2001, it was like losing a best friend. His play-by-play accounts of Minnesota Gophers football and basketball were legendary.

2. Al Shaver

Al was the voice of the Minnesota North Stars and a fan favorite for many years. He made you feel like you were sitting next to him in the booth.

3. Ray Scott

The legendary Green Bay Packers football announcer came here later in his career and did Minnesota Vikings football with former Viking Stu Voigt as the color commentator. Ray had a real flare for the pro game and was one of the best ever.

4. Herb Carneal

Twins baseball and Herb Carneal—they fit together for many decades. As with Ray Christensen, when Herb left it was like losing your best friend at the ballpark.

5. Frank Buetel

Frank was another of the legendary media men in the Twin Cities. He was the play-by-play man for Gophers football, was the first to do North Stars hockey on television, and did many state high school basketball and hockey tournaments.

MY 10 FAVORITE SPORTS MOVIES

I have been a movie buff for most of my life. My dad worked for Paramount films, and I have been caught up with the film industry ever since. I love all kinds of movies, from drama to comedy to musicals and just about anything else that comes along that seems worth seeing on the big screen. It's something about a comfortable seat, some popcorn, and the quietness of the theater that is inspiring. And given my line of work, I of course have some favorites in the sports-film genre.

1. *Raging Bull*

Who can ever forget Robert De Niro's searing portrayal of boxer Jake LaMotta? His performance was as good as any that has been seen on screen. Raging Bull is at the very top of my list of all-time favorite sports movies.

2. *Miracle*

This movie is very personal to me because I was in Lake Placid covering the game between the United States and Russia for WCCO television during the 1980 Winter Olympic Games. I know Herb Brooks was very proud to have Kurt Russell portray him in the movie. Every time I hear the movie soundtrack, I journey back to that little village in upstate New York.

3. *Field of Dreams*

"Dad, do you want to have a catch?" Every time I see this part of the movie, I go back to my childhood and playing catch with my dad. It doesn't get much better than that. Kevin Costner was terrific in the movie, which is an absolute delight for every baseball fan. It's one of those movies that simply gives you chills.

(Continued)

4. Bull Durham

Kevin Costner again, in one of the greatest films ever made. I loved it! Hilarious dialogue throughout and such great characters capture life in the minor leagues of professional baseball. The movie is a true classic in every respect. If it happens to be on television, you can take it to the bank that I will be watching it again and again and again.

5. Hoosiers

This incredible movie proves that dreams really can come true. It is an inspiring David-and-Goliath story of a small-time school reaching the Indiana state basketball championships. It features nothing short of exceptional acting by Gene Hackman and Dennis Hopper as well as a magnitude of thrills.

6. Brian's Song

I can remember sitting in my apartment crying my eyes out when Gale Sayers (Billy Dee Williams) sat at the bedside of dying teammate Brian Piccolo (James Caan). The emotion and passion expressed in the film was overwhelming. This was one of the first sports movies that brought this kind of passion and emotion.

7. Rocky

In all of my experiences watching movies, *Rocky* was the first and only time I've been in an audience that gave a film a standing ovation at the end. For anyone who sees this movie, I guarantee you will feel as though you are sitting ringside at the fight. Everything about the movie, including the soundtrack, was terrific!

8. *Slap Shot*

This movie was one of Paul Newman's best, and yet it was so out of character for him to play a foul-mouthed, brawling hockey player/coach. Of course, he starred along with the notorious Hanson brothers, who became famous in their own right.

9. *The Hustler*

Another Paul Newman masterpiece, in which Newman's "Fast Eddie" Felson takes on the legendary Minnesota Fats, played by the "Great One," Jackie Gleason, at the pool table. I have watched this movie over and over and over, and it gets better each time I view it.

10. *Tin Cup*

Yes, it is Costner again, in one of the very best films for anyone who has ever played or enjoyed the game of golf. It was 235 yards to the green and it took him 12 balls to get there. As each ball that Costner hits lands in the water, your hearts drop a little deeper.

MY **10** FAVORITE NON–SPORTS MOVIES

It's not all about sports for me. Here are my ten personal favorite non-sports movies, ones that I love and continue to watch any time I see them on television. I'm sure I missed a few, but these are the best of the best.

1. ***The Godfather***
Wow, what a film! I have watched it over and over and it always gets better. There are parts that still give me chills.

2. ***The Godfather: Part II***
This sequel is every bit as good as the first and gives me even more chills. It has incredible acting, a great cast, a solid plot, and everything else that made it and its predecessor box office hits and all-time classics.

3. ***Saving Private Ryan***
Tom Hanks was unbelievable, as were the other cast members. A real intense, heartbreaker movie. Simply one of my all-time favorites.

4. ***The Shawshank Redemption***
The inside of a prison is something most of us know very little about beyond what we see in the movies and on TV. I am told that this movie is very realistic in its portrayal of life behind the prison walls, much more than most.

5. ***The Dark Knight***
I love this big-screen presentation of Batman and his fight to overcome all that is evil. Our superhero lights up the screen!

6. ***One Flew Over the Cuckoo's Nest***
Jack Nicholson at his best. The story, the acting, and all that takes place is entertaining and powerful from beginning to end. Who's running the asylum anyway?

7. ***The Right Stuff***
Air Force test pilots and all that goes with their lives. The drama and cast are incredible.

8. ***Ferris Bueller's Day Off***
Really? Ferris Bueller? Yep, I'm serious. I get quite a kick out of this fun-loving movie. It's in my top ten, that's for sure.

9. ***Rear Window***
One of Alfred Hitchcock's best. Jimmy Stewart keeps you on the edge of your seat (a wheelchair, in his case). Loved all the drama and suspense! A blockbuster all the way.

10. ***Vertigo***
There are other Hitchcock specialties, but Vertigo is another of my favorites. Jimmy Stewart and Kim Novak—how could he go wrong making this film?

10 THINGS I WOULD HAVE DONE IF I HAD BEEN ELECTED GOVERNOR

As a part of the KQRS morning show with Tom Barnard, I ran for governor in 1986 and got—are you kidding me?—9,000 write-in votes! With the clout of the governor's office, I would change a few things. Don't worry about the timing of these events. We would make them happen.

1. Casinos in Downtown Minneapolis

We would have them in by now, and everyone would be having a great time enjoying losing their money. It just calls for that kind of action, and as governor, it would have been a slam dunk.

2. Expand Sports Gambling

Fix the roads! Fix the roads! Fix the roads! And where would all the money come from? That's right, sports gambling. All four-day fares go to Las Vegas and Minnesota, where the action is and the roads are great.

3. Transfer Sid to the *Pioneer Press*

I would have made a gubernatorial edict and moved Sid Hartman from the Minneapolis Star Tribune to the St. Paul Pioneer Press. It would have shaken things up a little in the sports world and kept things interesting. I'll have to ask Sid what he would have thought of me doing that.

4. Give Gary Anderson a Mulligan

He had not missed a field goal all season before that fateful afternoon at the Metrodome during the NFC Championship Game against the Atlanta Falcons in 1998. The missed kick by Anderson knocked the high-scoring, high-flying Vikings out of the playoffs. I would have issued a proclamation ordering an immediate rekick, a mulligan for Anderson.

5. Declare the Metrodome a Disaster Area

Yep, I would have done it. I would have made the declaration of "disaster area" to the worst baseball field, worst football field, worst stadium in the history of all high school, college, and professional sports. (Even though we have seen some pretty great things happen there!)

6. Place a Memorial at the "Take a Knee" Spot

Vikings fans will never forgive coach Dennis Green for his decision to have quarterback Randall Cunningham take a knee and let the clock run out at the end of regulation in the above-mentioned Gary Anderson game. So, in recognition, the spot of the knee would become an official state memorial for the Vikings faithful.

7. Select Amelia Santaniello as My Lieutenant Governor

No question about it, I would name my longtime WCCO colleague as my lieutenant governor. Amelia and I would work hard all day long doing all the necessary business for the state of Minnesota, and then rush off to do the 5:00 p.m., 6:00 p.m., and 10:00 p.m. news. It would have been a lot of fun!!

8. Throw the Flag

It was 1975 and the Vikings, with perhaps their greatest team ever, lost a highly disputed playoff game to the Dallas Cowboys at Metropolitan Stadium. The dispute came on a touchdown pass from Roger Staubach to Drew Pearson in the closing seconds. As every Vikings fan at the stadium or watching the game on television saw, Pearson pushed off on Vikings defensive back Nate Wright, knocking him to the ground and enabling Pearson to score the winning touchdown. "As governor of the state of Minnesota, I hereby order the official closest to the play to throw a flag, signifying offensive pass interference." How life would have changed for us all.

(Continued)

9. New Referees in Madison

I would have to order a replay of the infamous 1961 Minnesota Gophers football game against the Wisconsin Badgers in Madison. It was known as the game when the Jesse James gang showed up in Big Ten officials uniforms and stole the game from one of the greatest Gophers football teams of all time. All-American Bobby Bell's roughing-the-passer penalty followed by two consecutive 15-yard penalties on coach Warmath were instrumental in the Gophers' downfall.

10. Harmon's 500th Home Run

As governor, I would have ordered a huge press conference, with media from all over the country in attendance, to give the great slugger full recognition for his historic feat. Instead, Harmon got little attention, and he was disappointed in the Twins' loss that day. "The Killer" deserved more.

MY TOP 10 WCCO TELEVISION MEMORIES

I began my career at WCCO as a 17-year-old kid. I walked into the newsroom, sat down among the broadcast legends, and never left. I have been there for more than 40 years and have lived my dream ever since. It just doesn't get any better than what I have had—wonderful moments and wonderful memories. Here is a list of the best of them.

1. My Wife

It has been my best memory of all, because Denise and I met at WCCO television. She was an artist working on the night shift, and I recall thinking in the beginning, "Why is this beautiful woman talking to me?"

2. Dave Moore and the *Bedtime Nooz*

One of my most special moments at WCCO television was to be a part of Dave Moore's Saturday night program taping on my very first day at the station. I had just come in to observe, and next thing I knew, there I was working with the great Dave Moore. It was a thrill that has lasted my lifetime.

3. Slowest Elevator

I can remember people running the stairs to get to the set because the elevator took forever to get anywhere. There may be a new book out someday full of those old 'CCO elevator calamities.

(Continued)

4. First Basketball Show with Jim Dutcher

I don't think I have ever been as nervous as when I did my first show with Golden Gophers basketball coach Jim Dutcher. Jim could not have been nicer or helped me more. We had a marvelous time doing his shows, and it is one of my fondest memories.

5. All-Star Wrestling

They all came into the station for promo tapings. A 20-second sound bite from these guys has lasted with me for more than four decades. "The Crusher" was there and "Mad Dog" Vachon and all the others. I can remember Crusher saying, "I'm going to kill that . . . I'm going to tear his . . . " and on and on, and then he would say, "Did that sound okay?"

6. The Basement Newsroom

It was a smoke-filled, coffee-stained, cramped, crowded, desolate, isolated newsroom where legends were made. The absolute best of the best worked in this place, a collection of true hall of famers.

7. Hal Scott

Hal was my mentor and taught me so much. Whenever I hear his name, I can picture him wearing his traditional trench coat, with his weekend sport coat in a garment bag, and the cigarette. Hal will always be a legendary figure to me. He was the best!

8. Dave Moore

You want to talk about another legend? Well, that would be Dave Moore. Dave was so very special. He truly captured the community. He was our information source for news. I will never forget when Dave and I walked down the street in Minneapolis to a luncheon with the great Ted Williams. That day is captured in my memory vault forever.

9. My First Day at WCCO Television

I showed up with my $38 sport coat from the Fitwell department store, and I was hooked from the very first day I walked into the basement newsroom to observe. "I'll sweep the floor, pick up cigarette butts, wash the walls. Just give me something to do because I'm not leaving." I still feel that way today.

10. My Friends

"Work hard, play hard, and enjoy one another and what we do." This sentiment has held true for me over the past 40-plus years with all of the wonderful people that I have been associated with through the years at WCCO, from the early days and right through to today.

10 REASONS I LOVE MY JOB AT WCCO TELEVISION

The job at WCCO was made for me: I get to go to work every single day and cover sports. I could give many reasons why I love my job, but here are the top ten.

1. Every Day Is Different
No question about it: Every day on the job brings something different. When I leave for work in the morning, I never know exactly what we will be involved in that day. Every day being different makes the job interesting and exciting. It has been that way for me for more than four decades.

2. Surrounded by Great People
From the very beginning, the talent coming from the people that I am around is extraordinary. Exceptional people with great skills is the norm at WCCO.

3. I Get to See Joe Mauer a Lot
I'm sort of kidding with this one, but the fact is I have the opportunity to see Joe, and so many other great players, every day during baseball season. It's just amazing to have a job that puts me in contact with such tremendous talent and the greatest names in sports.

4. I Love Sports
I love sports, and covering sports is what I do for a living. It doesn't get much better than that.

5. The Press Box Food
I really love to eat, and I get to dig into the press box food at the games that I am covering—and it is good!

6. Complete Autonomy

I have had the good fortunate to pretty much be my own boss covering the sports scene. I do not have anyone looking over my shoulder telling me what to do and what to say. I have greatly appreciated the autonomy that I have had at WCCO.

7. Coworkers Are Like Family

Like I said earlier, I have worked with people who have great skills, but even more important in the big picture is that these coworkers are like family to me. We are great friends, and because of this my job is like an extended family.

8. I Get to Show My Passion

In my job, I get to really show how I feel about things on the air, whether things are going well or going poorly for a team or athlete or coach. I am a passionate person, and this helps me cover the sports scene and then report more than just the facts; I get to offer my editorial perspective.

9. Best Seat in the House

I wrote a book with this title because with my job, I truly do have the best seat in the house!

10. Teamwork at the Station

I love the relationship I have with my coworkers and all the talent that they bring to the station every single day. But I also appreciate the teamwork and the closeness that has been established. We work together closely, and in the process, we really do like each other.

INDEX